Gilson Ventura

The break with patriarchal marriage tradition

Gilson Ventura

The break with patriarchal marriage tradition

The Fifteen, Rachel de Queiroz

ScienciaScripts

Imprint
Any brand names and product names mentioned in this book are subject to trademark, brand or patent protection and are trademarks or registered trademarks of their respective holders. The use of brand names, product names, common names, trade names, product descriptions etc. even without a particular marking in this work is in no way to be construed to mean that such names may be regarded as unrestricted in respect of trademark and brand protection legislation and could thus be used by anyone.

Cover image: www.ingimage.com

This book is a translation from the original published under ISBN 978-613-9-67032-1.

Publisher:
Sciencia Scripts
is a trademark of
Dodo Books Indian Ocean Ltd. and OmniScriptum S.R.L publishing group

120 High Road, East Finchley, London, N2 9ED, United Kingdom
Str. Armeneasca 28/1, office 1, Chisinau MD-2012, Republic of Moldova, Europe
Printed at: see last page
ISBN: 978-620-8-10644-7

SUMMARY

To Gilmara, for her patience and understanding of my absences.

To my parents, for their example, strength and courage in adversity.

To my brothers and sisters, for their credibility and words of encouragement.

ACKNOWLEDGMENTS

To God, who in my weakest moments always encouraged me to keep going.

To Gilmara, who encouraged and supported me with her patience and words of faith.

To my parents and siblings, for their belief and trust that I would get here.

To my dedicated advisor, Prof.ª . Dr.ª . Terezinha Taborda Moreira, for her guidance and helpful teachings throughout this important period.

To my fellow master's students, for the dialogues and friendships gained throughout the course, who taught me a lot with their fantastic examples.

To all the professors of the Post-Graduate Program in Letters at PUC Minas, for their teaching during these two (2) years.

To all the secretariat staff of the Post-Graduate Program in Letters at PUC Minas who contributed to the completion of this work.

To the staff at the PUC Minas Library who were always on hand to find the books and information I needed for my research. To all those who directly and indirectly helped to make this work possible.

To CAPES for the scholarship.

"The representation of the world, as well as the world itself, is the task of men; they describe it according to their particular point of view, which they confuse with the absolute truth."

(BEAUVOIR, **The Second Sex: Facts and Myths**. [1949] / (1970), p.183).

SUMMARY

This paper aims to analyze Rachel de Queiroz's **O quinze**, written in 1930, in an attempt to highlight the questions it raises about the patriarchal system and marriage in Brazil at the beginning of the 20th century. This research will analyze the construction of the character Conceiçao, her relationship with her social environment and her possible romance with her cousin Vicente. Conceiçâo is a teacher who alternates her time between urban life at school and the northeastern countryside, spending her vacations at her grandmother Dona Inâcia's house in Quixadâ. In her professional and social journey, the character reflects on the impacts of drought and social inequality on the poor population of the Ceará backlands, taking a political stance towards them, while allowing us to reflect on the place of women in Brazilian patriarchal society at the beginning of the 20th century. For this study, theoretical sources were used that cover the relationship between literature and society, such as the reflections of Antônio Câdido; sources related to women's writing and feminism, such as the reflections of Simone de Beauvoir, and others linked to the construction of characters, such as the works of Beth Brait and Antônio Cândido himself. The research is bibliographical and exploratory, with recording, analysis, classification and interpretation of the data collected.

Keywords: Rachel de Queiróz, **The Fifteen**, women's writing, novel.

1 INTRODUCTION

- Love! This story of absolute, incoherent love is very hard to find... I, for one, have never seen it... What I see out there is a very obscure and timid instinct for closeness, which people obey as they see fit... I'm not speaking for myself... I don't even have that instinct... I'm sure I was born to live alone... (QUEIROZ, 2015, p.160).

O Quinze, a novel by Rachel de Queiroz published in 1930, became the subject of this work after long observations of the way in which Brazilian literature has portrayed the trajectory of the conquests of women's spaces, whether social, political or literary, which have expanded over the years, from Virginia Woolf, in **Um teto todo seu** [1929]/ (1985), to Simone de Beauvoir, in **O segundo sexo** (1970), up to the present day. The main concern that motivated this research arose precisely because of the observation of the great social advance that has taken place alongside the remarkable development of relations between women and those spaces that, for a long time, were dominated by men in an imposing way, due to patriarchy.

The novel is set in a period known in Brazilian literature as the Romance of the 1930s, between 1928, with the publication of José Américo de Almeida's novel **A bagaceira**, and 1946, with Jorge Amado's **Seara Vermelha**. This period is also known as the sugar cane cycle or the cycle of droughts in Brazil. The works published during this period have in common the denunciation of slave labor, prostitution and other social anomalies caused both by drought, in the specific case of the Brazilian Northeast, and by the social system in general.

It was during this period that Rachel de Queiroz emerged, whose writing would be considered one of the most representative of the period, becoming nationally known. Her fame soon reached the "masters of literature". By publishing a novel in her early teens, Rachel de Queiroz presents a character ahead of her time, Conceiçao, representing one of the feminine figures of the 1930s. Evidently, the work has an impact on the context of national literature; after all, a character from the backlands involved in reading Max Nordau, Ernest Renan and Pierre de Coulevain, among others, certainly incites some form of curiosity. As a result, the author began to be seen frequently in the literary environment, in cafés and in debates between intellectuals of the time. From then on, her involvement with the intellectual and political milieu was inevitable, culminating, however, in her imprisonment in 1932, due to her membership of the Communist Party.

Forty-seven years after the publication of **O Quinze**, in 1977, Rachel de Queiroz took up chair number 05 at the Brazilian Academy of Letters in Rio de Janeiro, which, since Machado de Assis, had only been occupied by men. For the time, this was something unusual and worthy of recognition. At the inauguration, the author quoted excerpts from a poem called "Plenilùnio" by Raimundo Correia, a poet she had admired since childhood, as follows:

In the white, moonlit room of the old farmhouse, a window is slowly opening onto the small enclosed garden, where there are carnations, bogaris and an orange tree. The little girl, more of a girl than a young woman, leans against the sill and searches for the moon with her eyes. She soon discovers it, so clear, you could read a letter!

The girl rests her myopic eyes on the moon, directly on the moon's disk. She sighs, but it's a different kind of sigh, satisfied, consoled; the girl is not yet at the age of proper sighs, she's at the age of imaginations and dreams. And with her eyes fixed on the moon, silently, barely moving her lips, she murmurs to herself a prayer, an enchantment - a poem? A poem that is both prayer and enchantment. He murmurs as if he were praying to the moon, and in fact he is praying to the moon:

... Star of the mad, sun of dementia Vara, noctambula aparição!

How many, drinking in your radiance How many, therefore, sun of dementia, moon of the mad, are mad!

You have already recognized the unforgettable poem in the enchantment prayed by the girl. And in the teenage girl who tries to make herself a witch of that lunar cult, allow me to introduce you to the old lady of today trying to unravel her ancient ties with the poem and with the great poet (QUEIROZ, 1977)[2] .

In her inauguration speech, as well as paying homage to Raimundo Correia, a poet she admires so much, the writer also pays tribute to several important names in literature.

The aim of this work is to study the way in which the narrator constructs the character Conceiçao and the way in which she breaks with a traditional marriage system long established by patriarchy. It's worth taking a step back in time and looking at the 1930s and the women's struggle to liberate women from the androcentric impositions that were so questioned at the time.

Eight years after the biggest literary event in Sao Paulo in 1922, called Modern Art Week, the early 1930s were still experiencing a hectic and, at the same time, promising atmosphere in the artistic and literary fields, a remnant of the event. Maria de Fàtima Salum Moreira (1997) makes an important record of how society behaved in the year that Rachel de Queiroz launched her first novel. In her work, Moreira (1997) shows that at the time there was a fierce social conflict between the male and female genders, which was recorded by the media.

In the same way, the newspaper **Apito**, although it was only inaugurated in 1932, two years after the book's release, was one of the major vehicles for propagating the conflicts between

---

2 As the information was taken from electronic media, it is not possible to indicate the page.

the two genres, which had obviously been going on since 1930. The editor of the newspaper created an entertainment page in which he answered letters from young female readers, but his prejudiced, pernicious and predatory responses to the readers were clear. On several occasions he addresses the female audience in an ironic way, clearly expressing this intention. And this irony with which not only this, but so many other media outlets dealt with the female figure was perfectly intelligible, and the intention was clear to try to silence the female voices that, on the contrary, every day found more space to make themselves heard.

Women's achievements were seen, for example, in relation to work and the right to vote. Although the CLT (Consolidation of Labor Laws) was only created in 1943, the Ministry of Labor predates the Consolidation, being created in 1930 and starting to regulate labor in 1934, i.e. before the CLT. So, while men already enjoyed some labor rights, women were still slowly moving towards a form of social recognition, which at the time was the right to vote from the age of 21. Diana dos Santos Ramos, who expertly studies the development of advertising in the 1930s, also adds that, with the development of the printed newspaper, with the aim of breaking with current concepts, there was an increase in the number of pages, because "society developed a lot, especially in urban centers. The increase in the production and publication of literary works during the decade shows a greater number of readers and, consequently, the general level of education of the population" (RAMOS, 2013, p. 62).

The female image began to circulate, showing women not as objects, as they had often been seen until then, but as subjects who acted and interacted with the world, quite different from the stereotype presented until then. In a commercial for automotive products taken from newspapers in the 1930s, presented by

Diana:

> The woman represented does not appear as a decorative figure or as an object of desire, but as a subject. There is no mention in the text of the need to justify the illustration, which suggests that it is common for automotive advertisements to feature the female figure as a driver, not restricting the world of cars to the male consumer. The text talks about the qualities of the products advertised, but the ad associates driving with a pleasurable activity also performed by women (RAMOS, 2013, p. 156).

Faced with a female behavioral picture as altered as the one presented from the 1930s onwards, marked by women's social advancement, it was not surprising that the patriarchy, shrewd and fearful, was frightened by such female resourcefulness. Perhaps (and here we come back to previous anthropological studies) the man of the 1930s was very afraid of the return of a social model of family observed by anthropologists from the work of Bachofen,

The Matriarchy (1987), studied here by researcher Martha Giudice Narvaz.

Analyzing Bachofen's work, it is possible to see the power that women once exercised in matriarchal societies. In her study, Narvaz highlights this model of society in detail. The researcher explains that: "Taking power, women instituted a new social organization called 'Gynecocracy', whose moral, legal and social values were based on the system of maternal law, structured around the figure of the mother-woman" (NARVAZ, 2005, p. 21, emphasis added).

What sparked this research into Rachel de Queiroz's narrative was the uniqueness of the fictional plot written by a woman that addresses the social and political problems of the Brazilian northeast, because the novelty was that it was a work of a social nature, narrating the great drought that occurred in 1915 in the northeast and the social ills written by a woman. Her portrayal of the concentration camps is something that greatly disturbs the political class and, since the work was written by women, it quickly became known in the artistic world.

O Quinze was written at a time of turbulent situations, not only in the social sphere, where discussions about the conquest of women's space were on the rise, but also in the political transformations mentioned above. The great influence and participation of the female class in this important period is analyzed, not only in literary activity, but also in political engagement, which was increasingly representative. And this transformation in the perspective of women's social participation led to enormous social and intellectual progress for post-1930 society.

The theoretical foundation that underpins this research includes studies by Antônio Cândido, when he addresses the society represented by literature, in his work **Literatura e sociedade** (**Literature and Society**) (2000), and research by Simone de Beauvoir, in her work focused exclusively on the female question, called **O segundo sexo** (**The Second Sex**) (1970). In addition to these, other theoretical underpinnings, such as those of Betty Friedan, Virginia Woolf, Constância Lima Duarte and Lùcia Castelo Branco were also used.

The research developed around the defined object is bibliographical and exploratory with recording, analysis, classification and interpretation of the data collected. Through induction, the literature was analyzed in both the general and specific areas of the topics covered. A more selective approach to the subject was also sought.

In its structure, this dissertation will present, after the introduction, an overview of the contextualization of the novel. Consideration will also be given to the characters in this fiction, looking for points of dialog between the 1930s context and the female characteristics expressed in the fictional text.

Chapter 02 begins the development of the body of the text, made up of three topics. In this chapter, entitled "Conceiçao: reflexões de uma normalista no sertâo", the dissertation focuses more specifically on the protagonist Conceiçao and how the narrator constructed her, shaping the character of the character who is going to break away from the oppressive patriarchal system. At first, Conceiçao is presented as an assiduous reader of works, including feminist and socialist tendencies, which is strange for her grandmother, Dona Inàcia, who represents the old patriarchal traditions in the novel. It is in this chapter that we analyze scholars such as Laile Ribeiro de Abreu, who argues that there is a subversion in the character, as she dedicates herself to "unusual readings for women of her time, has a job outside the 'home sweet home' and does not count on male protection" (ABREU, 2016 , p.12, emphasis added). Thus

In this subsection, we'll explain which of Conceiçao's traits contributed to her becoming a point of reference when we want to work on Rachel de Queiroz's other characters who didn't adhere to this slave tradition.

In chapter 03, entitled "Figurations of the feminine in **O Quinze**", the reflections are on the three types of representations of the feminine found in the work, which are seen from the three main characters: Cordulina, Mocinha and Conceiçâo. The aim is to demonstrate the main characteristics of each of these characters.

Chapter 04, "Women's writing in **The Fifteen**", focuses on women's writing itself, seeking to elucidate the differences and similarities between writing produced by women and writing produced by men. To this end, the research uses both theoretical and literary examples to demonstrate this discussion. Finally, the Final Considerations and References follow.

Faced with an important discussion that permeated the entire 1930s, around greater female participation in society, the work of Rachel de Queiroz is an indispensable work that complements the entire history of Brazilian literature. From 1930 onwards, any work dealing with the influence or otherwise of women in society and how their writing contributed to this influence will require reading Rachel de Queiroz's work.

2 CONCEIÇÃO: REFLECTIONS OF A NORMALISTA IN THE SERTAO

He picked up the first book his hand reached for, an old Polish story, a novel by Sienkiewicz, telling of heroics, rebellions and guerrilla warfare. Conce^ão leafed through it slowly, re-reading familiar passages, love scenes, duels, campaign episodes. He put it down and picked up the others - a volume of verse, a French novel by Coulevain. As he put them back on the table, he regretted it:

- This bookcase is very poor! I already have almost everything decorated!" (QUEIROZ, 2015, p. 10).

O Quinze, published in 1930 by Rachel de Queiroz, is a novel set in a period known in Brazilian literature as the Romance of the 1930s, a period of eighteen years between 1928, with the publication of José Américo de Almeida's novel **A bagaceira**, and 1946, with Jorge Amado's **Seara Vermelha**, a period also known as the sugar cane cycle or the cycle of droughts in Brazil. The works that span this period have in common the denunciation of slave labor, prostitution and other social anomalies caused by drought or even by the social system itself.

In addition to the novels already mentioned, others can be highlighted, such as **Sao Bernardo**, by Graciliano Ramos (1934); **Banguê**, by José Lins do Rego (1934); **Caminhos Cruzados**, by Érico Verissimo (1935); **Mar Morto** and **Capitaes da Areia**, both by Jorge Amado (1936 and 1937, respectively); and **Vidas Secas**, by Graciliano Ramos (1938). These novels also comprise what is known as regional literature, since they are set in a specific geographical location. Regarding this literary period, Antônio Càndido, a theorist who seeks to work with Literature as an instrument of social representation, states that:

> An interesting feature linked to the specific conditions of the 1930s was the expansion of regional literatures and their transformation into expressive modalities whose scope and meaning became national, as if they were coextensive with Brazilian literature itself. This is the case of the "novel of the Northeast", considered at the time by the average person to be the novel par excellence. Its vogue comes partly from the fact that it is rooted in the line of regional fiction (although not "regionalist" in the picturesque sense), now made with a previously unknown freedom of narration and language. But it also derives from the fact that the whole country has become aware of a vital part, the Northeast, represented in its living reality by literature (CÂNDIDO, 1989 , p. 185, emphasis added).

2.1 The Fifteen: a contextualization

Both in Brazil and around the world, the late 1920s and early 1930s were a period marked by a series of historical events that ended up being reflected in literature. One of the events that marks this period is the crash of the New York Stock Exchange in 1929, which left countless businessmen bankrupt. And in 1930, just a year later in Brazil, the 1930 revolution took place, marked by the rise of Getúlio Vargas and the end of the old coffee republic. It would be incomprehensible for the artists and intellectuals of the time to turn a blind eye to these facts and transformations. In view of the above, all the efforts for labor rights, the search for freedom and other manifestations were reflected on the pages of the novels, which sought to tell the story with a certain verisimilitude, composing themselves as social denunciation.

The verisimilitude stems from the fact that they are narratives about facts that, although they didn't happen, allow us to trace a plot that could have happened, as is the case, for example, with **O Quinze**. In this context, there is a real drought in the country, which can be seen in the annals of Northeastern history, so it is a real scenario, although the existence of the protagonist couple Conceiçao and Vicente is not real, nor are the other characters, who are relevant to the plot, even though they were inspired by real people. In this context, the novels' character of social denunciation does not alter the reality of the facts, and this is what characterizes the Realist Novel of the late 19th century, which leads some critics to call the 1930s period Neorealism.

So, although until the first decades of the 19th century there were some women who wrote and left their legacy in writing, it was unusual to think of women occupying the places where literature circulated. During this period, the "literary pen" remained predominantly in the hands of men, who held the power of the written word in their hands. Constância Lima Duarte observes that:

> Most people thought that it was enough for a girl to know how to embroider, cook and play the piano. The first legislation authorizing the opening of public girls' schools dates back to 1827, and until then there were only a few convents that kept girls for marriago, privatc schools in the homes of teachers, and the option of individualized teaching, preferred by wealthier families. And it was the first "educated women" of the time who took it upon themselves to extend the blessings of knowledge to their fellow women, opening schools, publishing books, and confronting the current opinion that insisted that women didn't need to learn to read, let alone write (DUARTE, 2011, p. 74, emphasis added).

Although the context was 1930, with literary dominance practically in the hands of men, in the midst of this amalgam, along with the "barons of literature", a woman emerged, Rachel de Queiroz, whose writing will be considered one of the most representative of the period. Her contact with the literary world expanded nationally with the publication of her first novel, **O Quinze**. With its publication, the work put the writer in the spotlight at a time when little was said about women's writing in Brazil and what was said always came with certain reservations.

Given these two contexts, social and literary, and in dialogue with both, the novel **O Quinze** can be divided into two planes. The first is marked by the emotional relationship between the protagonist Conceiçao, an educated teacher, and her cousin, the cowboy Vicente, a rough man, as the narrator defines him: "a friend of the bush, of the sertâo, of everything that was uncultured and rough" (QUEIROZ, 2015, p. 19). The second is marked by the trajectory of the cowboy Chico Bento and his family, struggling against the misery imposed by the drought in the sertâo.

At first, Conceiçao is presented as an avid reader of works, including feminist and socialist tendencies, which makes her grandmother, Dona Inàcia, a representative of the old patriarchal traditions in the novel, feel strange. Conceiçao spent all her holidays at the family farm in Logradouro, near Quixadà. Although she was twenty-two, she wasn't thinking of getting married, but she did have a somewhat compromising relationship with her cousin Vicente. With the onset of drought, Dona Inàcia decides to move to the city and leave Vicente to take care of everything. Bravely resisting the drought, the boy works tirelessly to keep the animals alive. Meanwhile, Conceiçao decides to take part in voluntary work at the concentration camp where the dying migrants from the devastating drought are housed. In her reflections, the girl realizes the ideological difference between her and her cousin and the near impossibility of a more affectionate relationship with the boy. The drought ends and they return to the village.

Secondly, the narrative presents the tragic and painful journey of the cowboy Chico Bento, his wife Cordulina and their five children, representing, in the novel, the migrants who wandered through Ceará at the time of the drought that hit the region in 1915. The family is forced to leave the farm where they live and work. To do so, they save some money and buy supplies and a donkey to cross the sertao, with the intention of working in the north, extracting rubber. During the journey, a dramatic event, common during the drought, befalls the Bento family: the couple lose Josias, their youngest son, who poisons himself with "wild" manioc and dies in agony. His end is poetically described by the narrator:

> There Josiah had stayed, in his grave by the side of the road, with a cross of two sticks tied together, made by his father. He was at peace. He no longer had to cry from hunger on the road. He no longer had a few years of misery ahead of him, only to fall into the same hole, in the shadow of the same cross (QUEIROZ, 2015, p. 70).

Another common occurrence in the backlands of Ceará during the drought is what happens to poor Chico Bento. Faced with excruciating hunger, the man ends up killing a goat he finds along the way, only to discover later that it had an owner. The owner called him a thief and took the rest of the goat home, giving Chico Bento and his son, who was with him at the time, only the animal's entrails to satisfy their hunger. Leagues later, Chico Bento realized that his eldest son, Pedro, was missing. Arriving in Acarape, where he thought he might find him, he saw an old friend, his compadre, who was then the region's delegate. They receive some supplies from him, but are unable to find his son. They learn that the boy had run away with a group of cachaça dealers. When they arrive at the concentration camp, Chico Bento's family is recognized by Conceiçao, also his comadre. She suggests Chico Bento for a job and, in the end, he adopts one of her children, Duquinha, as well as advising them on how to buy a train ticket benefiting from the government, which enables them to travel to Sao Paulo, no longer working with rubber, which was their initial intention. To the disappointment of the readers, the romance between Conceiçao and Vicente doesn't materialize and the last scene of the two of them has a tone of an unfulfilled prospect:

> The boy saw his cousin, blew on the animal and took off his hat in a broad gesture: - Good evening!
>
> Lourdinha even shouted a message to her mother. Vicente put his spurs to the horse, which took off in a great rush. And Conceiçao watched him disappear into the golden fog of the night, galloping like a ghost through the shadowy shape of the hills (QUEIROZ, 2015, p. 162).

After the release of the book, Rachel de Queiroz became nationally known. The novelty of her work was that it was social in nature, narrating the great drought that occurred in 1915 in the Northeast. As well as depicting social problems, it also discussed the tradition of marriage through the character Conceiçao, and was a feminine piece of writing. The aesthetic treatment through which her writing portrays the concentration camps ended up upsetting the political class at the time. Written by a "female pen", the work circulated quickly in the artistic milieu, given its innovative nature. At that point, everyone wanted to know who Rachel de Queiroz was. At first, the book didn't attract much attention in Fortaleza, as the author herself tells us when she says that "they even wrote an article saying that the book was printed on inferior paper and didn't say anything new" (QUEIROZ, 1998, p. 31). Her biography even includes a comment from Graciliano Ramos, who, on reading the work, spoke with suspicion about female authorship:

> It came out of the blue in the mid-1930s and did more damage to spirits than José Américo's novel because it was a woman's book and, what was really astonishing, about a new woman. Was it really about a woman? I didn't believe it. After reading the volume and seeing the picture in the newspaper, I shook my head: There's no one with that name. It's a joke. A girl like that doing a novel! It must be the pseudonym of a bearded guy (RAMOS, 1980, p. 137).

On the advice of Rio de Janeiro journalist Renato Viana, Rachel sent the "little book" to Rio de Janeiro, where it achieved notoriety, beating the works of the male writers who had preceded her. From then on, the author pursued a brilliant literary career after 1930. By publishing a novel in her early teens, featuring a character as ahead of her time as Conceiçao, who came to represent the dissatisfaction with which many women lived in the 1930s, Rachel came to be noticed in the literary environment. Her involvement with the political milieu was inevitable, culminating in her imprisonment in 1932, due to her participation and great influence in the Communist Party, which she left after her release from prison.

2.2 Conceição: the character

Conceiçao is a character who questions marriage, motherhood and the family. Thus, it is curious and ironic to think that the name Conception incorporates a meaning of responsibility and commitment to marital relations, being of religious origin, which comes from the Latin *Conceptus,* meaning fruit or conception, as well as being one of the titles attributed to the Virgin Mary, such as Our Lady of the Conception. It is also related to the "immaculate conception of Jesus Christ", since Mary, according to Judeo-Christian tradition, would have conceived without marital relations, the original sin.

The name Conceiçao was brought to Brazil by the Portuguese colonizers and many indigenous people and African slaves received it when they were baptized by the catechizing priests. And as we'll see later, although Conceiçao renounces marriage and biological motherhood, she ends up fulfilling the role of mother by adopting Duquinha, the son of the retreatant couple Cordulina and Chico Bento. Her subversive intent thus seems to be linked much more to marriage itself than to the concept of family itself, as Laile Ribeiro de Abreu points out:

> There is a subversion that already emerges in Conceiçao, the protagonist of *O Quinze*, as she denies marriage and motherhood, dedicates herself to unusual reading for women of her time, has a job outside of "home sweet home" and does not count on male protection, since there is no reference to her father, whom she lost at an early age, and almost no passage that recalls her grandfather, with the grandmother being the only mark of her descent (ABREU, 2016, p. 12, emphasis added).

At the beginning of the novel, Conceiçao is introduced to the reader in a domestic setting. The narrator makes a point of portraying her first scene inside the house. It is important to note, however, that although she is in this environment, her actions are not those of a person who acts according to this place, like her grandmother Mâe Nàcia, the nickname by which Conceiçao addressed Dona Inàcia, by whom she was raised. Already in the first scene of the novel we can see the contrast between Conceiçao's characteristics and those of her grandmother:

> After blessing herself and kissing St. Joseph's medal twice,
>
> Dona Inàcia concluded: "Deign to hear our supplications, O most chaste spouse of the Virgin Mary, and obtain what we pray for, Amen." Seeing her grandmother leave the sanctuary room, Conceiçao, who was braiding her hair, sat in a hammock in the corner of the room and asked her:

- And it rains, huh, Mother Nàcia? It's the end of the month... Not even for your novena...

Mrs. Inàcia raised her confident eyes to the roof:

- I have faith in St. Joseph that it will still rain! We've seen winter start as early as April.

On the large dining table, where a red checkered tablecloth stretched out, two cups and the teapot, under the embroidered muffler, announced supper.

- Aren't you coming for your latte, Conceiçao? The girl finished her braid, got up and began to eat, silent, abstracted (QUEIROZ, 2015, p. 09).

Here, we see a prototypical "housewife" grandmother, a religious woman who prayed for help and made a point of serving the family at mealtimes, which was her tradition, certainly passed down from generation to generation. Conceiçao's critical speech, quoted above, shows us how much the character viewed her grandmother's belief and devotion with a certain amount of disbelief, uncertainty and even irony. When we think about this speech and link it to the scene in which Conceiçao chooses a book from her grandfather's bookshelf to read, we can better understand the great influence this library had on the character's upbringing. The scene allows us to understand that the grandfather was a freethinker and had already published a work of a religious nature:

He got up and went back to the cupboard. He came back with a thick bound volume with the name of his late grandfather, freethinker, Freemason and hero of Paraguay, in gold letters on the spine. It was a treatise in French on religions. Yawning, he began to leaf through it. But little by little, something interested her. And, lying down, in the red light of the lighthouse, which was blackening the top of her sleeve with black smoke, in the calm of the sertanejo night, while in the next room her grandmother, insomniac as always, fiddled with the beads of her rosary, Conceiçao became immersed in the descriptions of rites and mystical descriptions, and spelled out the harsh names with which God was invoked throughout the lands of the world (QUEIROZ, 2015, p. 11).

Right from the start, the narrator reveals signs of how her character's profile refers to a spirit that is much more inclined to break with the tradition that Dona Inacia had kept up until then than to perpetuate it, something that will become clear throughout the book. Conceiçao's comment reflects her reading, so discriminated against by her religious mother Nacia, who always referred to it in an innocent and pejorative way, saying that "this girl has some ideas!" (QUEIROZ, 2015, p. 12).

When the narrator informs us that Conceiçao would sometimes quote Nordau or Renan from her grandfather's library, and shows this critical nature of her grandmother's religiosity and some interest in religious treatises, it is possible, through reading, to evoke one of the most famous works by Ernest Renan, a French historian read by Conceiçao: *The Life of Jesus (Origins of Christianity),* first published in 1863. Although he doesn't deny the existence of a man called Jesus, his work tends to humanize the Jesus preached by religions, oscillating between human and divine history, while demystifying the latter. This tendency can be seen when he states, for example, that:

> Almost all the miracles that Jesus thought he had performed seem to have been miracles of healing. [...] In such a state of knowledge, the presence of a superior man, treating the sick person with affection, giving them the certainty of their recovery by means of some sensitive signs, is often a decisive remedy. The Essenes, who are so closely related to Jesus, were also considered to be very powerful spiritual doctors (RENAN, 2004, p. 257-260).

Despite the length of time between the two generations that separate Conceiçao and Dona Inacia, it cannot be categorically stated that these differences can only be explained by a generational conflict. The reading with which Conceiçao occupied herself can be seen as one of the main factors responsible for forming in Dona Inacia's granddaughter such ideas that were so rejected and foreign to her.

By introducing the two characters into the novel in this way, the narrator skillfully and subtly shows the reader the profile of each of the characters, informing them about one of the grandmother's habits, that of serving, and about one of Conceiçao's habits, that of reading, already foreshadowing who the reader will meet. This strategy of the narrator, of allowing the reader to perceive the character's traits through her habits, is similar to what Beth Brait (1985) develops when she equates the narrator with cameras through which the characters are captured. Thus, "the third-person narrator [...]", says Brait, "[...] simulates a continuous record, focusing on the character at the precise moments that interest the progress of the story and the materialization of the beings that live it" (BRAIT, 1985, p. 56).

The novel stands out not only because it deals with the issue of the social problem that occurred in the year that gives it its title, but also because, concomitant with the problem of drought, it brings up the discussion of female emancipation, with Rachel de Queiroz's first character to make this debate possible. Queiroz's character, at a time when women were struggling to free themselves from the "strong hand" of the patriarchy under which they lived - a patriarchy which, in turn, realizing the imminence of its downfall, tried at all costs to maintain its cloak of superiority, at a time when women were being presented with various emancipatory routes - will allow her to debate various phenomena linked to the female question, given her intellectual training, which made her a woman of critical and subversive thought. Her reflections will go through the extreme poverty caused by the drought of 1915, the questioning of the blatant social difference that existed at the time, marriage as the basis for imprisonment in a monogamous family and the dependence of this family model on patriarchy.

When studies and reflections are made about the character Conceiçao and, more specifically, about her abnegation to marriage, it can be seen that, as well as revealing, in Queirose's work, the social problems of the sertão caused by the drought, she is responsible for breaking with the institution of marriage. In doing so, Conceiçâo demonstrates that, beyond marriage, there are other possibilities for women to achieve happiness that are not limited to the marital union, which many previous literary works insinuated, corroborating the idea of marriage as the only way to achieve happiness, which involved a veritable marriage trade, fueled by the existence of the dowry paid to the groom for his yes at the altar.

The next characters in Rachel de Queiroz's works to follow in Conceiçao's footsteps are Santa, from **Joao Miguel** (1932), who leaves her husband for the character Corporal Saul, and Noemi, presented in the third novel **Caminho** de **pedras** (1937), a married woman who, after getting involved with Roberto, a friend from a political party, leaves her husband Joao Jaques. It is true that in both novels the form of subversion takes place under different conditions. Although the characters don't renounce their marriage, their "subversive" reactions, to use a term coined by Laile Ribeiro de Abreu (2016, p. 12), are the breaking of the union already established by the altar vows. If Conceiçâo inaugurates what we are calling a break with the patriarchal marriage tradition, what can we say about Maria Moura, Rachel de Queiroz's last novel? Maria Moura not only escapes these stereotypes, she manages to have at her command a band of men, jagunços, servants of all kinds who obey her in everything she needs. It was a requirement of the matron that, when she recruited her henchmen, they should be on standby:

- I'll warn you: it might be worse with me than with a corporal and a sergeant.

They have to obey me with their eyes closed. They have to forget that I'm a woman - that's why I'm wearing these men's pants. Beating my chest:

- There are no women here, only your boss. If I tell you to shoot, you shoot; if I tell you to die, you die. Anyone who disobeys will pay dearly. So dearly and so quickly that they won't even have time to repent (QUEIROZ, 1992, p. 57).

And so it was that Maria Moura made her way to the Serra dos Padres and built her fortress, which was her initial goal. The men accompanying her really did seem to forget that she was a woman, so strong was she. Rachel de Queiroz called her "The Lampiona of the Northeast". And it's no wonder that Queiroz went on to say, in an interview with the Moreira Sales Institute's **Caderno de Literatura Brasileira**: "My women are crazy, aren't they? Perhaps it is resentment of what I am not and would like to be" (QUEIROZ, 1997, p. 26).

As for the influences suffered by the character Conceiçao, the narrator doesn't tell us anything about her childhood, she doesn't give us any family reasons why she felt against tradition or marriage itself. What she does tell us is that a large part of her ideological formation came from the influences she acquired in her grandmother's library, which was at odds with the prevailing culture for women at the time, and here we are referring to the traditional culture exercised by marriage. This culture is the same one imprinted in the words of her grandmother Mâe Nàcia, when she said that "a woman who doesn't marry is a cripple" (QUEIROZ, 2015, p. 11). These words, spoken by her grandmother, criticize the fact that Conceiçao had reached the age of "twenty-two and there was no talk of marriage" (QUEIROZ, 2015, p. 11).

And it is precisely this character's firm position of not wanting to get involved with someone who wasn't "worth it" (QUEIROZ, 2015, p. 136), which will make her a representative of the break with this tradition, the main point worked on in this research. It cannot be said, however, that Conceiçao did not dream, at some point in her life, of forming a family or even getting married, as her reflections on the figure of her cousin Vicente are contrary to this statement. However, when asked about her postponement or self-sacrifice to be with someone, her answer was

was emphatic: she hadn't found anyone who was "worth it":

- Mother Nàcia, when you give up certain obligations, home, children, family, you have to find other things to worry about...

Otherwise life becomes too empty...

- And what have you twisted your nature into? Why don't you get married? Conceiçao gave her grandmother a sly look:

- I never found anyone worthwhile... [...]

- I asked what was the reason for his abstraction?

- I was thinking that Lourdinha is very happy... The boy hinted at a flirtation:

- But, Mrs. Conceiçao, you don't have the same happiness because you don't want to... Conceiçao laughed:

- Who told you?

The young man twirled his moustache with his big hand, and his little eyes twinkled with mischief:

- Oh, I draw my own conclusions... For myself and for others... Conceiçao laughed again:

- But I never found anyone who was worth it (QUEIROZ, 2015, p. 136 - 160).

In this way, Conceiçao put off the idea of marriage. She was a quiet, homely girl and her cousin only aroused certain feelings in her because of the intimacy and closeness between the two of them since she was a child. There are no scenes of flirtation between Conceiçao and other men in the novel, except in the scene at the Quixada Christmas party, where the dentist insinuates a quick flirtation which Conceiçao promptly dodges, saying that mother Nacia is calling her, leaving the dentist alone.

The character's entire trajectory in the novel, which, as we have said, makes her the first and most important Queirosean character to represent what we are calling a "break with the patriarchal marriage tradition", imbues her with a certain greatness of spirit, a greatness that will be directly linked to the model of discussion that the character allows to take place throughout the history of women's participation in Brazilian literature. With regard to this greatness of spirit, what Antônio Càndido says is of great importance:

> The greatness of a piece of literature, or a work, depends on its relative timelessness and universality, and these in turn depend on the total function it is capable of exercising, detaching itself from the factors that tie it to a particular time and place. This function is apparently less pronounced in oral literature, which seems to be limited to the restricted scope of the groups in which it operates and which produced it. [...] The social function (or "sociological raison d'être", to speak like Malinowski) includes the role that the work plays in establishing social relations, in satisfying spiritual and material needs, in maintaining or changing a certain order in society (CÂNDIDO, 2000, p. 41, author's emphasis).

It is clear that patriarchy had already been discussed and questioned before Rachel de Queiroz's work. However, the social context of the 1930s, a period in which patriarchy was being vehemently questioned, meant that a narrative like **O Quinze**, written by a woman, came to be considered, as it was, a work that would achieve the timelessness and universality of which Antônio Càndido speaks. Its repercussions point to these conclusions.

2.2.1 Based on tradition

When Antonio Cândido lists the most common types of sociological studies in literature, he presents at least six types, of which the second type, explained by the critic, is of interest to this study:

> In order to establish ideas and delimit areas, we can try to list the most common types of sociological studies in literature, carried out according to more or less traditional criteria and oscillating between sociology, history and content criticism. A first type would be made up of works that seek to relate the whole of a piece of literature, a period, a genre, to social conditions. A second type could be formed by studies that seek to verify the extent to which works mirror or represent society, describing its various aspects. This is the simplest and most common type, basically consisting of establishing correlations between real aspects and those that appear in the book (CÂNDIDO, 2000, p.11).

Cândido exemplifies this type of modality with "W. F. Bruford's study of the fidelity with which the Russian society of *Chekhov*'s time is represented in his plays and short stories (*Chekhov and his Russia*)" (CÂNDIDO, 2000, p.11). His reflection makes us think of the denunciatory and representative motto in Rachel de Queiroz's novel, in which not only the relationship between the people of the Northeast and drought emerges, but also, and this is one of the points that stimulates this work, the reflection on the relationship between women and society in the 1930s and that society's view of marriage, plus the defense of women's obligation to give in to every patriarchal whim and imposition in a passive and unquestioning way. When we look at the history of Brazilian literature, we find some authors engaged in social and political issues in which various institutions are inserted, marriage being one of them. Brazil's extensive literary heritage regards marriage as something fundamental, crucial and sacred, so that renowned and consecrated authors always take great care when it comes to breaking with this tradition. Of course, this kind of break doesn't consolidate dizzily from one decade to the next.

In his work *The Origin of the Family, Private Society and the State,* Engels discusses this phenomenon called tradition in an investigative way. He states that until the end of the Middle Ages "marriage remained what it had been since its origin: a contract not signed by the parties concerned" (ENGELS, 1884, p. 84). Then there were group marriages, in which individuals were born attached to a particular group or syndicates[3] :

> Such was the situation that capitalist production found itself in when, from the age of geographical discovery, it set out to conquer world domination through universal trade and manufacturing industry. It must be assumed that this form of marriage suited him exceptionally well, and this was indeed true. And yet - the irony of world history is unfathomable - it was precisely capitalism that opened up the decisive breach in this mode of marriage. By transforming all things into commodities, capitalist production destroyed all the old traditional relationships and replaced inherited customs and historical rights with buying and selling, with the "free" contract (ENGELS, 1884, p. 85, emphasis added).

With regard to this type of monogamous marriage investigated by Engels, what can be observed about its effect on the situation of women is that the more established monogamy becomes, the more patriarchy advances and establishes itself, imprisoning and dominating not only women, but also their children. In a more in-depth study, Claudia de Jesus Maia (2007), developing her thesis in search of answers about the dominance of patriarchy, makes her forays into demystifying patriarchy, removing its "savior of the fatherland" mantle. Maia states that:

> In this process of convincing women to adhere to normative, modern conjugality (indissoluble monogamous

3 In the abduction of women, there are already indications of the transition to monogamy, at least in the form of syndiasmic marriage; when a young man, with the help of his friends, abducts a young woman by force or seduction, she is possessed by all of them one after the other, but then becomes the wife of the promoter of the abduction (ENGELS, 1884, p. 10).

marriage, based on mutual obligations), one of the discursive strategies used was to create the idea of exclusive privileges or rights for the wife, such as the free choice of her own husband, romantic love as the basis of marital relations and the rational government of the modern home (MAIA, 2007, p. 106).

In the words quoted by Maia (2007), we can see the astute interest of the patriarchy which, in collusion with capitalist interests, sought domination not only by implanting a tradition, but by manipulating the manifestation of a greater feeling that was supposed to direct marriage, which was love. Now, if at a given moment the patriarch tries to impose love by determining who the daughter or son should or shouldn't marry, by allowing the girl or boy to choose their own partners in monogamy, aren't the "owners of the girls or boys" dictating when they should love?

Rachel de Queiroz's character Conceiçao seems to know all about this constructed form of love. She suspects that behind this feeling there is a larger entity: capitalism, which drives it. She used to say:

- Love! This story of absolute love is incoherent, it's very hard to find... I, for one, have never seen it... What I see out there is a very obscure and timid instinct for closeness, which people obey as they see fit... In fact, I'm not speaking for myself... I don't even have that instinct... I'm sure I was born to live alone... (QUEIROZ, 2015, p. 160).

By breaking with the millennia-old tradition of marriage, Conceiçao not only questions marriage itself, but the next "sacred" institution that extends from it, considered the *maternal* cell of society: the family. In addition, in a more subtle way, through her voluntary work in the concentration camp in support of the retreatants there, she makes a social critique when she shows, denounces that what should be done by the State was done by people like her, who, in the short moments of rest from their work, left the comfort of home to spend their time in favor of the disadvantaged and neglected by the State. Her appearance when she arrived from the countryside was a clear sign of her position, to which the narrator draws the reader's attention, as follows:

When she crossed the gate of the Field and leaned against a post, she breathed a little easier. But even from the outside, there was a stench! [...] I left home at ten o'clock and finished school at two. From school I went to the concentration camp to help deliver aid. Her eyes were sore from the sight of so much misery, and she wouldn't arrive until late in the evening, exhausted, recounting sad scenes that would also fill her grandmother's glasses with water (QUEIROZ, 2015, p. 65; 80).

Conceiçao's haggard appearance thus expresses, far beyond the character's simple altruism, her practical way of contesting a system that is negligent and omits the forgotten in those fields, without the slightest condition for survival. Thus, the character goes beyond the discussion of marriage and opens up a broad discussion that reflects the great transformation that the female class was going through in the 1930s.

2.3 Vicente: friend of the bush, of the sertâo, of everything that was uncultured and rude

Studying the history of the formation of the state of Cearà, one of the issues that stands out is the research carried out into the main crops from which the state developed:

> Cotton cultivation, which was then widespread in Ceara, was joined by charqueadas (activities linked to the consumption of meat), forming the basis for Ceará's economic and spatial organization. In this sense, the system formed by the cattle/cotton/subsistence crop tripod not only structured Ceará's spatial economy, but also profoundly marked the distribution of funds and the use of land in the state (RUFINO apud PEREIRA JÙNIOR, 2003).

These were then the state's main crops, the basis of its economy, and the main producers were involved in them at the time. It is in this context that the character Vicente finds himself, setting out to develop one of these crops, raising cattle in the northeastern highlands, resilient and persevering, since he is one of the few who won't let his cattle go, as Mrs. Maroca from Aroeiras had done, as can be seen below:

> The old woman shook her head in amazement:
>
> \- And you won't give up! Haven't you thought about retreating to the mountains, or doing like Maroca, letting go and letting die? Vicente stood up, a little excited:
>
> \- No, ma'am! I won't let go of any of them even if I run out and lose all my money buying lumps!
>
> I've already started, I'll finish! Drought also has an end... (QUEIROZ, 2015, p. 82).

One can see in the boy's speech his determination to take care of what belonged to him on the farm, and he disapproved of his neighbor's attitude when she let the cattle go, abandoning them to their fate. Vicente was the oldest of the men in the family. His younger brother was inclined to study and had graduated with a bachelor's degree in Rio. He lived in Cariri with his wife and mother-in-law, "finding the sertão life 'an ignominy', 'a degredo', and his only ambition was a public job in the capital" (QUEIROZ, 2015, p. 20, emphasis added). At first, Vicente's lack of interest in literature caused some embarrassment in the family, which naturally subsided over time. Insinuations about the young man's choice always came from his father's remarks "when he said, in conversation: my son, the doctor..." (QUEIROZ, 2015, p. 48).

Vicente had a close relationship with Dona Inàcia and Conceiçâo. His comings and goings at Dona Inàcia's house in Logradouro always left the girl restless and pensive after he left. She thought about everything, her cousin's habits, comparisons with her brother Paulo and, above all, what would become of him if they were to form a family. From an early age, there was a closeness between her and the boy that only the two of them and, of course, a more attentive reader, could detect. And it was this veiled relationship between her and her cousin that made them think so much about the possibility of forming a family, even though they had never expressed such an intention.

And it was Vicente's fondness for "all that was uncultured and rude" that caused the girl a certain apathy and made her so pensive after the boy's visits (QUEIROZ, 2015, p. 19). Since she was a reader, as already mentioned, of writers such as Nordau, Renan, Couvelain, or even Machado, she saw a real intellectual gulf between herself and her cousin, which perhaps forced her to attempt a less banal dialog between the two, since Vicente had already stated, without the slightest regret, that "of books, only the cattle note..." (QUEIROZ, 2015, p. 87). Faced with the boy's spontaneity and conformity in not dealing with letters, Conceiçao felt a certain fear at the thought of marrying that matuto, as she pondered:

> What a strange couple they would be when, in the evenings at the farm, she underlined a happy thought in a beloved book and wanted to share the impression she had received with someone. Perhaps Vicente would look up and murmur a distracted "yeah" to her from behind the newspaper... But of course, how far away and with how much indifference... She thought that even the powerful charm that his healthy fortitude exerted on her would not bridge the tremendous gulf that separated them (QUEIROZ, 2015. p. 88).

Although the narrator doesn't explicitly open up to the reader the romantic interplay between Conceiçao and Vicente, she builds up this closeness between them step by step and the reader comes to understand it. Two scenes are shown from which it is possible to clearly perceive what is happening between the two young people, considering that, in a normal relationship, jealousy, with a good measure of moderation, is totally welcome, as Thiago de Almeida reminds us, citing Kingham and

Gordon:

> Of all the types of jealousy mentioned in scientific literature, romantic jealousy, i.e. that which occurs in romantic relationships, is one that has attracted the most attention from psychologists and laypeople alike. Among the most differentiated of human emotions, jealousy is extremely common. [...] According to some theorists, it is inherent, that is, constitutive of human nature, so that we are all jealous to a greater or lesser degree (ALMEIDA; CENTEVILLE, 2007, p. 01).

In the two scenes of the novel that follow, jealousy can be seen in the characters' attitudes. She, in a more authentic and demanding way, and he cunningly, without fully showing what is going on inside him. On one of his trips to the concentration camp in his work helping the displaced people, Conceiçao meets a girl called Chiquinha Boa, who lives on the land where Vicente's farm is located. In conversation with the girl, Conceiçao doesn't miss the opportunity to hear from his cousin. When she hears about the boy's isolation, she feels sorry for him until the girl says: "- Not at all! Vicente is a very fun person... He's a hard worker, but he's always chatting to one person and another... He's a very unkind young man... He's just a prose writer..." (QUEIROZ, 2015, p. 64). This comment from Chiquinha Boa bothers Conceiçao. The girl even talks about Vicente's possible involvement with a girl from the farm, Josefa. As she listens to the story, Conceiçao shows signs of discontent that the reader cannot escape:

> Conceiçao let her talk, and Chiquinha continued with a malicious laugh:
>
> - And even that daughter of Zé Bernardo's, just because he always stops by and says a few words to her, she's acting all cool - Conceiçao found the story strange and couldn't help himself:
>
> - Does he have anything to do with her? The mulatto shrugged: - People are very ignorant... If he does, so much the worse for her... That white boy isn't for a goat's beak like us...
>
> The conversation began to bother Conceiçao; the stench from the field seemed more intense, and he stood up, handing the woman a silver:
>
> - Tomorrow I'll come back and see how you're doing - I come here every day to help deliver the aid... If you need anything at all, ask me and I'll do what I can...When she crossed the Campo gate and leaned against a post, she breathed a little easier (QUEIROZ, 2015, p. 65).

Later, in a conversation with Mâe Nàcia about what happened, the narrator goes into an important question about the conflict between her generation and her grandmother's generation. When she angrily tells her grandmother about the conversation she had with the girl in the field, Conceiçâo becomes even more enraged by Mâe Nàcia's observations, which show, without any astonishment, enormous conformity with the occurrence of the event:

> - Chiquinha also told me something funny... Funny, no... silly... "She says they're talking a lot about Vicente with Zé Bernardo's Josefa..." [...] Dona Inàcia looked into the past and remembered an old time when she too had had those outbursts and revolts... And in the end, it's all natural and to be expected, and you get used to it by force... She tried to console her granddaughter, who was returning to her room:
>
> - My child, life is like that... Since the world was a world... I even think today's men are better.
>
> Conceiçao turned around quickly:
>
> - Not me! I die and I can't get used to it! That's right! Look, Mâe Nacia, I could like a person as much as I liked, but knowing a story like that, there was no saint that could do that! (QUEIROZ, 2015, p. 69).

In this speech we can already see a break with the tradition of marriage in Conceiçao, because from the moment she demonstrates her concept of love and the marriage relationship, the enormous difference between what she thinks and what her grandmother thinks becomes evident. After all, her grandmother used to say that Conceiçao had "strange ideas". Her grandmother's response makes Conceiçao search through her reading for the real reason for this subordinate characteristic infused into poor Mother Nàcia's mind,

And the girl compared Dona Inacia to those blue-souled ladies that Machado de Assis talks about[4] ... It was then that she remembered that Vicente had probably never read Machado... Or anything she read. He always said that, of books, only the cattle note... In a stronger relief, as strong as she had never felt it, the difference between them, in taste, in tendencies, in life, became apparent (QUEIROZ, 2015, p. 87).

Faced with this realization, Conceiçao vehemently refuses to follow the same path as her grandmother, in other words, to be one of those "blue-souled women that Machado talked about" (QUEIROZ, 2015, p. 87). On the contrary, "knowing a story like that, there was no saint that could help" (QUEIROZ, 2015, p. 69). After Conceiçao's encounter with Chiquinha Boa in the concentration camp, there is a noticeable distance between her and Vicente, which is felt throughout the text until the final moment, when "she saw him disappear into the golden fog of the night, galloping like a ghost through the shadowy figure of the hills" (QUEIROZ, 2015, p. 162).

The second scene in which jealousy is perceived, this time from Vicente's point of view, proving that the narrator is building up this relationship in a discreet and tenuous way, takes place during one of the young man's trips to town to buy feed for the cattle and stop by Dona Inàcia's house. Conceiçao was still at school or perhaps in the concentration camp, as she almost always left school for the countryside to help deliver aid. Vicente kept talking to Dona Inàcia, waiting for the girl to arrive, until he couldn't stand his curiosity and anxiety about the delay any longer and asked: "Why doesn't Conceiçao show up?" (QUEIROZ, 2015, p. 82). Dona Inàcia explains the girl's altruistic behavior. After Conceiçao's arrival, after the formal greetings, a dialogue begins between her and Vicente until, at a certain point, the boy's jealousy and annoyance become clear, as can be seen below:

Seeing her finish reading and close the letter, he laughed:

- When you came in, Aunt Inacia was saying that she wasn't expecting you until the afternoon.

- Ah! It was because I had a massive headache today, and I didn't go to the camp... But just seeing you here made me feel better...

Vicente laughed, shaking his head. Then he asked seriously:

- Was it because of the illness that came alone? She laughed again:

- Alone? I'm always alone! I'd have to see if I could find company every time I went to school...

- Because I thought it wasn't customary for a girl to walk alone in the city. [...]

---

4 In **Esaù and Jacó** we learn about the drama of brothers who fall in love with the same woman, which will be the main thread of the whole novel, causing a quarrel between them. The mother, Natividade, one of those women with a blue soul, will suffer until the hour of death, begging the brothers to reconcile: "She wiped her eyes with this green handkerchief, and she would have other handkerchiefs if the one she had was torn or stained; one, for example, not green like hope, but blue like her soul" (ASSIS, 2012, p. 61).

- But it's because I'm an old teacher that I go to work! A pretty girl doesn't just go for a walk, does she?

He said he was still carried away by his matuto zeal.

- Even so, being an old teacher, as you say, if I told you to, I'd only let you leave with a band guard... (QUEIROZ, 2015, p. 83).

The two scenes, as well as demonstrating the construction of the character Conceiçao as an independent woman, even with a male companion by her side, because, after all, someone who already works outside has the right to answer for herself, show the gradual decay of patriarchy, represented by Conceiçao's irony when she disdains and dismisses a male companion to walk with, even though she claims to be an "old teacher". In this way, this decadence is reflected in the pages of Rachel de Queiroz's literary writing.

2.4 The blue-souled ladies of Machado

By mentioning the "blue-souled ladies of which Machado speaks" in the first scene, Conceiçâo sets a precedent for reflecting on a question that permeates the entire novel, which is also the intention of this work to discuss, since we believe it is also the author's intention to discuss the issue of female subalternity. Although in the work cited by Conceiçao, **Esaù e Jacó**, it is not the author's interest to talk exclusively about the same subject, we are very interested in his approach based on the character Conceiçao. Even though Machado didn't create his character Natividade, from **Esaù e Jacó**, from the stigma of a subordinate woman, since that wasn't his intention, Wagner Martins Madeira (2001), analyzing her, observes that Natividade, "Machado's blue-souled woman", as Conceiçâo says, is "the ideal woman with her blue soul" (MADEIRA 2001, p. 110). And in the context of Machado's work, as well as Rachel's, it doesn't take much effort to understand that the ideal woman to whom the author refers is the woman who lives in conscious subalternity to the man. The precedent that Conceiçâo sets is an opportunity to reflect on Rachel de Queiroz's work in the light of the thoughts of the Indian writer Gayatry Spivak, who makes a *sui generis* reflection on subalternity in her work **Can the subaltern speak**? (2010), which is very useful for our reflection. Reflecting on the condition of the Hindu widow, who self-immolated on her husband's funeral pyre[5] , Spivak observes a curious fact that demonstrates the dominance of patriarchy in the affirmation of female subalternity. According to the scholar, in her investigation of written records in search of this recurring phenomenon in India, she finds that:

---

5 The Hindu woman climbs onto her dead husband's funeral pyre and immolates herself on it. This is the widow's sacrifice. [...]. The ritual was not universally practiced and was not relegated to one caste or class. The abolition of this ritual by the British was generally understood to be a case of "white men saving dark-skinned women from dark-skinned men". (SPIVAK, 2010, p. 94).

The testimony of the women's voice-conscience is never found. Such testimony would not have been ideological, transcendent or "totally subjective", of course, but it would have constituted the ingredients for producing a counter-sentence. Looking through the grotesquely poorly transcribed names of these women - the sacrificed widows - in the police reports included in the records of the East India Company, one cannot single out a voice. The most that can be noted is the immense heterogeneity that

It goes through such a skeletal and ignorant account (Castes, for example, are usually described as Tribes) (SPIVAK, 2010, p. 94).

Thus, in the name of subservient domination, the patriarchal system causes the figure of women to be somewhat erased and silenced. We can see that this silencing is being transferred to the pages of literature, as the author herself explains above when she looks for records of Hindu women who self-immolated on the funeral pyre. The author notes that "looking through the grotesquely poorly transcribed names of these women [...] one cannot single out a voice, [...] One never finds the testimony of the voice-consciousness of women" (SPIVAK, 2010, p. 94). From this, the scholar concludes that the writings around this ritual were strictly conducted along an androcentric and tendentiously meticulous line. When talking about the "Hindu manipulation of the constitution of the female subject", Spivak states that:

Between patriarchy and the formation of the object, the figure of the woman disappears, not in an immaculate void, but in a violent throw that is the displaced figure of the "third world woman", trapped between tradition and modernization (SPIVAK, 2010, p. 119, emphasis added).

And if there is no complete disappearance of the figure of the woman, as Spivak (2010) shows, there is at least a way of silencing her. Since the question of the silencing of women in literature has been mentioned, Terezinha Taborda Moreira (2016), in the wake of studies by Sandra M. Gilbert and Susan Gubar (2000) on the stereotypes of the angel and the monster through which women are represented in Western literature, recalls that:

In both situations, women are left with a condition of silence. Whether she is a reader or a writer, silence is what the patriarchal, phallocentric society imposes on her and expects of her, since her possibility of expressing herself is limited to incorporating the masks with which she is spoken (MOREIRA, 2016).

One could venture to say that not only in the two situations to which Gilbert and Gubar refer, but judging by Spivak's unsuccessful search for records of the female pen on the sacrifice of Hindu women, perhaps not in the two situations cited alone, but in three. After all, as well as encountering problems with the issue of silencing in reading and writing, as the writers say, we are faced here with yet another form of silencing: representation, because, in a true opportunism in representing women, in fact the representation of women by the pen of patriarchy is something complicated, as will be seen below. If not complicated, at least questionable.

3 FIGURES OF THE FEMININE IN THE *FIFTEEN*

"The intellectual woman as an intellectual has a circumscribed task which she must not reject as a frill." (SPIVAK, 2010, p. 126).

Several theoretical and literary debates have already argued about the fact that women's history is represented under the pen of patriarchy[6] and how this representation can be questioned because it contains, between the lines, the harsh shadow of prejudice and the interest, albeit veiled, in maintaining the trait of subordination and curbing female emancipation that has so frightened the phallocentric domination since the first feminist manifestations. We intend to develop the issue of women's writing in more detail in the next chapter. However, we can already see, from the narrator's construction of the characters' profiles, the peculiar representative character that each of them will take on.

It can be seen in the book that the narrator constructs at least three types of representations of female profiles, each with its own particularity. Taking into account what we want to work with as a representation, the first type of representative aspect is that which is instilled in the construction of Conceiçao herself, the girl who "was twenty-two and didn't talk about getting married" (QUEIROZ, 2015, p.11). In other words, Conceiçao is the one who comes closest to this phenomenon of breaking with tradition that we have been working on throughout this research.

The second character is Mocinha, Cordulina's sister, who, at the first signs of freedom, is enchanted by the possibility of getting to know the world outside the sertâo, because when she heard about the possibility of working, "Mocinha arrived excited, laughing" (QUEIROZ, 2015, p. 56). Stuck with the only model of life she knew, that of subservience to the hardships of the sertâo, to the sadness that the misery of the drought imposed on them, Mocinha glimpsed the offer of work at the station. Even though it was underemployment, the idea of being able to be among the different people she would be passing through enchanted her. In this way, Mocinha will represent the possibility of the existence of another post-drought world, unlike the many women whose only world away from the sertâo that they could see was that of the concentration camps that housed the skeletal people suffering from the drought.

And finally, there is the one who comes closest to the female prototype that would represent the model of woman that patriarchy sought to preserve: Cordulina, a woman who is at her

6 In chapter two, we discussed Spivak's critique of the ritual of women sacrificing on the funeral pyre. According to her: "The testimony of the women's voice-consciousness is never found. Looking through the grotesquely poorly transcribed names of these women - the sacrificed widows - in the police reports included in the records of the East India Company, no (female) voice can be singled out" (SPIVAK, 2010).

husband's side come rain or shine, after all, "Cordulina lowered her head, Chico Bento kept talking" (QUEIROZ, 2015, p. 32). By referring to the character in this way, the narrator expresses, in a synthetic and faithful way, the profile of the woman who most contributed to the perpetuation of the patriarchal system that prevailed in the 1930s.

From this perspective, by arranging the three characters in a given order of representation and assigning them a meaning that encapsulates the essence of their representativeness, we can apply a division that is configured as follows: the idea of *subordination* is contained in the representation of Cordulina, due to her total surrender to the commands of her husband Chico Bento, since, of the three characters, she is the one who most assumes this posture of patriarchal subservience, subordinating herself to the dictates of this system, represented by her husband; the idea of a *dream* is contained in the representation of Mocinha who, from the beginning of her journey, behaves like a woman with a vision that stands out from the others, because she sees the possibility of knowing other horizons beyond the great sertão that surrounds and oppresses the sertanejos; and the idea of *emancipation* is contained in the representation of Conceiçâo, to the extent that the character breaks with the patriarchal system. In each of these ideas you can find the essence of these characters that Rachel de Queiroz draws in an extraordinary way in the figures she proposes for the feminine in her writing.

3.1 Cordulina

Cordulina, Chico Bento's wife, is a very important character in the novel. She is presented, at first, as a fragile and lamenting figure, and then, gradually, it is revealed, through her, how strong the sertanejo woman is who resists, with great firmness and maturity, the loss of two children in the sertâo, to poverty. She is also the companion who, in her husband's moments of weakness, will strengthen him, helping him to reflect on his weaknesses. She is the one who will put up with her husband's truculence in his hours of revolt. Initially, she can be seen as a weak creature, fearful of the adversities of life and of being. There is great fear in the character, for example, when she says to her husband: "But, Chico, I feel so sorry for my little shack! Where are we going to live in this world of my God?" (QUEIROZ, 2015, p. 32).

In a second moment, however, it is possible to see the character getting stronger and gaining body during the walk in scenes such as the moment when, after much crying, Cordulina acquires a certain resistance, as the narrator shows in the following excerpt:

> Cordulina was hardly crying anymore. Perhaps it was even for the boy's happiness. Where could he be in greater misfortune than staying with his father? [...] Cordulina didn't cry any more. The day before, when she had gone to say goodbye to Duquinha, she seemed to have run out of tears; and with dry eyes she stared at

the waves that came and went crashing against the iron pillars (QUEIROZ, 2015, p. 122).

In this scene, we can see that what the poet Carlos Drummond works on in one of his great poems**, The Feeling of the World,** is being fulfilled**:**

There comes a time when you no longer say: Oh my God

A time of absolute purification [...]

And the hands weave only the rough work. And the heart is dry.

Your shoulders support the world

And it weighs no more than a child's hand (ANDRADE, 1999, p. 23).

Drummond's poem explains how suffering seems to corrode human feelings so that they can no longer be felt. We no longer understand what is happening to human beings when they are consumed by time, which is "absolute purification". The heart no longer feels and life becomes an obligation, without any form of satisfaction with the shoulders supporting the world.

One of the aspects that makes Cordulina stand out is her choice to be silenced throughout the novel, making her another important character to contribute to the rupture that Conceiçao represents. Before her departure, when the reality of the drought imposed on the suffering sertanejo people was not yet clear, the character still has a voice. In the scene in which Chico Bento tries to collect the tickets that the government was distributing to people leaving the sertão, Cordulina intervenes before her husband arrives:

- How did you do, Chico? Did you bring the money and the tickets?

- What passages! Everything has to go overland, like an animal! Who can find anything in this mess! God was only born for the rich!

Cordulina saw by her husband's breath and the fury of his apostrophes, so unaccustomed to his quiet nature, that he had had too much to drink, and she questioned him:

- But, Chico, what do you take it for when you go to Quixadà? Every time you come from there it's like this!

- Nonsense, woman! I took nothing! I killed the bug! What I wanted was to be really drunk, to forget about all the misery!... (QUEIROZ, 2015, p. 36).

That was the Cordulina that came out of the serum. Another was the Cordulina we see in the sertâo. When working on silencing in Conceiçâo Evaristo's Poncia Vicêncio, Cristina Felipe Ribeiro states that voluntary silencing is a way of getting in touch with the void, and "To get in touch with the void is to dialog with the mysteries that words cannot reach; we are not dealing with alienated subjects, but with alienated ones. In Poncia's case, as she gets closer to her ancestry, to the figure of her grandfather, she withdraws into silence."

(RIBEIRO, 2016, p. 66).

Cordulina retreats into silence as she becomes aware of the reality of crossing the sertão to try and reach "Sao Paulo" (QUEIROZ, 2015, p. 120). At first, "Cordulina listened and opened her heart to that hope". (QUEIROZ, 2015, p. 32). Later on, we find Cordulina "lowering her head and Chico Bento continuing to speak". (QUEIROZ, 2015, p. 32). Even before her departure, when she sees her husband trying at all costs to convince her that the best thing to do is to leave the sertâo, Cordulina, somewhat incredulous, already begins to understand the uselessness of her opinions in the face of an austere and obstinate husband. In the serão, watching her son Josias who had poisoned himself, "Cordulina cried without consolation". (QUEIROZ, 2015, p. 61). Cordulina begins to feel the hardships of the pain of sertâo. The pain of losing her first child has already made it impossible for Cordulina to argue against the living and sad drought, which will intensify with the loss of her second child, because "Cordulina listened confusedly to what they were saying, and cried quietly". (QUEIROZ, 2015, p. 92). The woman understood the strength of resistance in her silencing, because when she realized that her son was missing, "Cordulina hardly cried anymore". (QUEIROZ, 2015, p. 94).

Thus, the woman finds in silence her way of resisting the impositions of the terrifying system that forces her to leave her place, where until then she had found a certain security, to go after her husband to an uncertain and insecure place.

3.2 Mocinha

In this study of the novel **O Quinze**, it can be seen that few scholars give any kind of emphasis to the character Mocinha, Cordulina's sister who lives with the couple. Given the motivations that the girl shows during her departure from the sertâo, we can consider her an idealist, even in the midst of the precarious possibilities that the sertanejo environment offers her.

Without the slightest raw material, Mocinha built herself a world of ideals far away from that rink. We don't know where she got so much hope from. Laile Ribeiro de Abreu (2016) argues that Mocinha's journey from the sertao ends up "bringing her closer to the reality that lies ahead of her, de-characterizing her from any idealization, re-signifying her in a more human position" (ABREU, 2016, p. 198). At a certain point, during the family's journey, Mocinha's appearance becomes increasingly disfigured by fatigue, hunger and the scorching midday sun of the sertao. At this point, Chico Bento quips: "Hein, my comadre! You've put luxury on the back burner..." (QUEIROZ, 2015, p. 44). In relation to this observation by Chico Bento, Abreu states that:

> Abandoning luxury means taking on her role in the journey that is part of her life and the lives of those who share this dry walk with her, towards a thread of hope that comes to the retreater in settling in a place that has not luxury, but water. Mocinha's humanization occurs when she takes on this role and subjects herself to the dust of the road and her sister's help with the children, giving up the dreams of a girl her age (ABREU, 2016, p. 198).

Although we have this aspect of the character Mocinha, later on we realize the true intention of the narrator in building a character with so many dreams, even in the midst of conditions as inhospitable as those of the sertão. Alongside her sister, we know that the girl had no prospects whatsoever. Even so, the sad situation doesn't take away her desire to dream. A scene that faithfully shows us this quality of the character is the moment when the narrator describes her in a different way in which, even as they set off on the long walk out of the serão, "Mocinha, in her starched dress, also carried her bundle under her arm, and in her hand, her red slippers from going to mass" (QUEIROZ, 2015, p. 41).

The term "slippers for going to mass" is reminiscent of the tradition of the great sertôes and small inland areas, where the best garments are reserved for the Sunday of mass. Both Chico Bento and Cordulina show sadness and uncertainty about the future when they leave the sertão. However, Mocinha doesn't show these feelings, she is a character who nurtures a certain expectation in the face of events. This hopeful character can already be seen in her tranquillity and confidence as soon as they leave the serão:

> Chico Bento, intervening, climbed the smaller one. And the others, behind their father, took their revenge, sticking out their tongues with insulting gestures, but they were lost because the knight didn't see them, immersed in the joy of his victory. Suddenly, his little voice broke into a heartfelt cry:
>
> - Look at Rendeira!
>
> And he pointed to a cow painted black and white, which, thin and quiet by the side of the road, seemed to be waiting for the fugitive family to say a final goodbye. Cordulina started crying again; Chico Bento himself quickly wiped his sleeve across his face. Rendeira stared into all of his big, painful eyes, from which a clear stripe ran down his dark muzzle like a trail of tears. Only Mocinha looked at the reindeer with indifference, fixed her slippers in her hand and continued walking with her soft step, so fast and light that it barely crushed the crumbly clods on the ground (QUEIROZ, 2015, p. 42).

The narrator describes the character's optimism and vanity and then goes on to criticize one of the most terrible forms of domination in the patriarchal system: the girl is the victim of abandonment after an unwanted pregnancy that turns her into a beggar. The violence suffered by Mocinha is not just physical, but mainly psychological and social.

The fact is that Mocinha, like many other women, had always dreamed and ventured out to get a job, an activity from which she could earn her own living, just like Conceiçao. However, coming from a precarious sertâo and without any life experience, she allows herself to be seduced by the charms of a man and her end is to be the mother of a son abandoned by a father of whom the readers are not even aware.

Overwhelmed by the possibility of being able to interact with people other than those poor creatures of the sertão, Mocinha surrenders more and more to the spontaneity of the conversations, which ends up leading to a disagreement with her boss and her definitive abandonment of her job. Now, truly alone, with no relatives, far from home and far from Conceiçao, she has no choice but to wander the world without knowing which direction to take. His last appearance in the novel is narrated from his meeting with Dona Inàcia at the train station. On meeting her during a journey to Baturité, Dona Inàcia doesn't recognize her:

> Bless you, Madrin'Nàcia!
>
> On the station platform, a thin, dirty, ragged girl - one of the eternal ghosts of the drought - clutched a wandering parcel in her lap and whimpered softly.
>
> Dona Inacia didn't recognize her:
>
> - Who are you?
>
> The girl clung to the edge of the car and moaned sadly:
>
> - Doesn't Madrin'Nàcia know me? I'm Mocinha, Chico Bento's sister-in-law, from Aroeiras...
>
> The old woman put her hands to her face in dismay:
>
> - You! But young lady, what was that?
>
> - Woe betide you, my godmother! Chico had left me in Castro, at the house of a woman who sells at the station. But I didn't put up with it and I was passed around from hand to hand, getting worse every day, until I ended up in this mess, and with a child at my breast... The poor thing isn't even a month old yet.... I don't know how I didn't die, out there in the open, suffering everything I needed... (QUEIROZ, 2015, p. 152-153).

Despite the precarious living conditions in which the girl found herself, the greatest misfortune that surrounded her was the great prejudice that an unmarried and pregnant girl faces in the context in which the character was inserted. When we analyze Mocinha's situation, we see that the character is the protagonist of the social criticism made by Max Nordau, the author read by Conceiçao, as the narrator tells us in at least two moments of the narrative. The first occurs when the narrator presents Conceiçao's intellectual characteristics, stating that: "in fact, Conceiçâo might have had some ideas; she was writing a book on pedagogy, had scribbled two sonnets, and sometimes she happened to quote Nordau or Renan from her grandfather's library" (QUEIROZ, 2015, p. 12). The second occurs when the narrator shows how Mother Nàcia feels uncomfortable with her granddaughter's reading:

- And are these books any good for girls to read, Conceiçao? In my day, girls only read novels that the priest told them to... Conceiçao laughed again:

- This isn't romance, Mother Nacia. Don't you see? It's a serious book, a study book...

- What's it about? You know I don't understand French... Conceiçao, faced with this unexpected listener, tried to summarize the theme of the work, naively trying to steer her grandmother towards her own ideas (QUEIROZ, 2015, p. 135).

There are at least two clues in the scene that lead the reader to infer that the serious book to which Conceiçao refers is Nordau's book. At first, Conceiçao tells her mother that it wasn't a novel but a "serious study book" (QUEIROZ, 2015, p. 135) and the grandmother complains to her granddaughter that she can't read French. In 1883, Max Nordau published one of his most famous works in Paris, **The Conventional Lies of Our Civilization**, in French. The immense success of the work elevated him to the level of a celebrity.

In the book, one of the conventional lies Nordau works with is the "marriage lie". The author is deeply critical of what he calls conventional marriage, a marriage made solely for the sake of shady financial and social interests. Although in his work the author directs his criticism more towards European countries, it is known that the phenomenon he discusses is not restricted to these countries, but in Brazil, there are periods in which this practice even inspires Brazilian authors to deal with the subject, as is the case with the novel **Senhora**, by José de Alencar. On this subject, Nordau states that:

Conventional marriage, i.e. the nine-tenths of marriages contracted among the civilized peoples of Europe, is therefore a profoundly immoral and fatal situation for the future of society. Sooner or later, it brings those who perform it into conflict between their sworn duties and their indestructible love, leaving them with only the choice between degradation and destruction. Instead of being a source of rejuvenation for the species, it is a means of slow suicide for it (NORDAU, 1950, p. 208).

The author also talks about what he calls love without marriage and its product: children. At the same time as drawing attention to the children of *loveless marriages* as "despicable creatures", he also draws our attention to the children generated through *lovelessness*, in other words, a relationship that didn't go through the common procedures of society, that is, it didn't go through the priest. Regarding children born out of wedlock, the critic states:

The offspring of love without marriage are all victims of their mothers' social proscription and become martyrs to the dominant prejudices. [...] The feeling of solidarity that belongs to their primordial instincts, like that of all higher animals, degenerates (NORDAU, 1950, p. 209).

From the perspective presented by Nordau, which apparently guides the construction of the character, Mocinha was reserved, without the slightest shadow of a doubt, for the social proscription mentioned by the author, and to see her son succumb in that rink would be a fate just like that of her sister's children, whom she had seen left behind in the desert, lost or found by death. By reflecting on the problem of the representation made by the young girl in the novel, the narrator allows Nordau's voice to echo and become proficiently recognized, creating a dialogical polyphony between the novel and the theorist's work.

3.3 Conception

The construction of the character Conceiçao is marked by her main attributes. Among them, her relationship with the intelligentsia, her altruism (through her work with the concentration camp inmates) and her contact with her grandfather's library serve to lead to a possible diagnosis of who this important Queirosean protagonist, who influenced so many characters after 1930, might be. In relation to this construction, we should also talk about the issue of motherhood in the work.

If Conceiçao, with her act of renouncing marriage, affirms to the phallocentric domain her independence and her not needing marriage to be happy, she complements her message by extending this independence to the way she chooses to exercise motherhood: by adopting a child and, from this act, performing a maternal function without the need for male intervention that this would provide her.

"Being a mother" has long been questioned by some scholars, including Elisabeth Badinter, who, by researching maternal love since before the 17th century and well into the 20th century, developed an enlightening study of the many problems intrinsic to this phenomenon, giving rise to the work **A love conquered: the myth of maternal love** (1980).

In her work, Badinter tries to show that just as marriage was shrewdly molded to meet the interests of capitalism and its development, motherhood had the same biased and cruel course. Through an accurate study, the author analyzes the way in which some women simply didn't give a damn about having a child and how this was something perfectly natural in 17th century French society.

This shows how motherhood is worked into a woman's consciousness to the point where the fact of not having a child becomes something shameful and humiliating for her. Many women who, in the middle of the 20th century, love their unborn child unconditionally, never imagined (or can imagine) the indifference to which many newborns were subjected two or three centuries ago in France. Thus, Badinter states that:

> The apparent absence of grief at the loss of a child is not an excuse for parents. Mothers have identical reactions. Shorter quotes the testimony of the founder of an asylum for found children in England, who was

shocked by the mothers who abandoned their dying babies in the streams or on the garbage heaps of London, where they were left to rot. Or the jovial indifference of a member of good English society who, "having lost two of her children, observed that she still had a dozen thirteen left". [...] In his thesis, F. Lebrun writes: "On a human level, the death of a child is felt as an almost trivial accident that a later birth will repair." [...] But there is no greater proof of indifference than the absence of parents at their child's funeral! In certain parishes, such as Anjou, no parent would bother to attend the funeral of a child under five. In other parishes, sometimes one of the parents attends, sometimes the father (BADINTER, 1980, p. 88-89, emphasis added).

In the current context, we know that while many fathers still carry, to a lesser extent, the legacy of paternal neglect observed in France in Badinter's studies, others regret the "bad luck" of not being able to give birth to a child, due to some biological problem or not, leading to the current adoptions. Others, even though they are not victims of any problem, moved by a greater altruistic feeling, adopt children and love them with the same intensity as if they had given birth to them. This is the case of Conceiçao, who, although she had no problem with her ability to gestate, ended up adopting a child.

Although this attitude of adoption was not something premeditated, but happened as part of the work of building the character, in the first chapter it is noted that, when reproached by her grandmother about her reading, Conceiçao tells her that "when you give up certain obligations, home, children, family, you have to find other things to worry about... Otherwise life becomes too empty..." (QUEIROZ, 2015, p. 136). At this point in the narrative, Conceiçao doesn't imagine, and neither does the reader, that soon afterwards she will adopt a child and, as well as spending her time reading Renan and Nordau, she will have a child to look after.

When she adopts Duquinha, Conceiçao will, at first, take on the role of mother that her mother was unable to do due to the problems caused by the drought, and she will do so in a way that is as loving to the child as her own biological mother would have been. This loving dedication to the child is similar to what Badinter says about wet-nurses who, after years of dedication, finally decided to adopt the child they had breast-fed, so attached was the child to them:

Several of them were very attached to the children they were breastfeeding and refused to go home to be with them. More attached to these children than to their own children, is it any surprise that they prefer to live in a bourgeois home, where life is softer for them than in their own home? Over time, the foster family becomes their real family (BADINTER, 1980, p. 232).

By adopting the son of Cordulina and Chico Bento, Conceiçao begins to play a role with all the affective peculiarities of a mother, because from the start she shows total attachment to the boy. When the couple were about to leave for São Paulo, as they were planning to do,

Conceiçao showed how attached she had become to the child, rejecting the idea of giving him back to his mother by saying: "Ah! This is mine, I'm not giving him away anymore, I'm going to make a man out of him! No, comadre, you can't take that one!..." (QUEIROZ, 2015, p. 118).

In this adoption, we see the same process that Badinter questions in her work: to what extent is bearing a child an essential condition for "being a mother"? When she sees her sister-in-law Lourdinha at the kermesse, the girl at first seems to give in to sadness when she sees her happy with her first child. However, when she sees Duquinha, her adopted son, approaching, her feeling of emptiness dissipates, as she sees in the boy the fulfillment of her dream of being able to nurture and care for a child just like her sister-in-law.

In this way, Rachel de Queiroz's work addresses the possibility of women occupying a place in society that differs from the traditional rite, that of following a certain model imposed by social dictates that completely ignore women's happiness and comfort. In Conceiçao, there is a break not only with the traditional pattern of the woman who is obliged to marry, but also with the prejudice against women who, not having a child to breastfeed, are seen as spinsters deprived of maternal power.

Badinter's studies thus go on to demystify the true dogmas that maternal love ends up instilling in society, observing various situations with the aim of proving the fragility of this love, stating that "everyone knows that love is not expressed all the time, and that it can persist in a latent state. But if we don't take care of it, it can weaken to the point of disappearing" (BADINTER, 1980, p. 15).

In her studies, the anthropologist argues that there were cases in which children were born to be left with third parties, and only came to enjoy contact with their mothers after four or five years. She also demonstrates that maternal love is an optional love, or a love induced by patriarchal discourses at the service of the capitalist system. To this end, her studies go beyond the power of the state and reach the ideological arguments of the church to show that, since the High Middle Ages, the Roman Church has proclaimed equality between men and women, because, according to Badinter (1980), the teachings of the Church express that "the message of Christ was clear: husband and wife were equal and shared the same rights and duties in relation to their children" (BADINTER, 1980, p. 30).

Looking at the Roman Church's view of the issue of offspring, the author argues that patriarchal power grew disproportionately to that of women, supported by the institutions of church and state, to the point where "in the 13th century, the father could still kill his son without suffering serious consequences. This power was, however, endorsed by the mother herself, in addition to these institutions which were increasingly involved in the governance of the family" (BADINTER, 1980, p. 31). This scenario could be perceived and experienced more precisely in the south of France as early as the 17th century, as the author states:

> The power of the husband and father far outweighed love. The reason was simple: the whole of society rested on the principle of authority. Three discourses intermingled and helped each other to justify the principle and the facts: that of Aristotle, who demonstrated that authority was natural, that of theology, which affirmed that it was divine, and finally that of the politicians, who claimed that it was divine and natural at the same time (BADINTER, 1980, p. 31).

While patriarchal power was growing, another phenomenon was taking place alongside it: women's interest in reading and intellectual growth. This growth worried and threatened the foundations of the patriarchal system. Elisabeth Badinter (1980), speaking of Robert Bray and his work **La préciosité et les précieux** (1951), which observes Parisian women in their first manifestations of intellectual interests, draws attention to what Bray says about the Parisian women Cathos and Magdelon, who, without any concern, openly declare themselves opposed to the "mediocrity" of domestic life. As a result of their declarations in French society, there was a considerable drop in the weight of traditional family values, which earned them a certain amount of rejection from some. They had "stubborn adversaries among the bourgeois, so well described by Molière, attached to traditional values: the Sganarelle, Gorgibus or Chrysale" (BADINTER, 1980, p. 108). Badinter also reiterates that:

> These women needed a lot of courage and perseverance to read the forbidden books. Not that they risked much by defying the prohibitions, but they had received such a mediocre education, not to say nothing, that we are surprised by their intellectual ambition. And finally, their achievement. Sometimes more vain than cultured, the dream of a women's academy excited them more than hard intellectual work. Their enemies took advantage of this weakness and mocked it by exaggerating it (BADINTER, 1980, p. 109).

Sganarelle, Gorgibus or Chrysale were some of the enemies "who considered women to be nothing more than the first slaves of their houses, and forbade their daughters to read any books other than those they used to pray to God" (BADINTER, 1980, p. 109). It is through these arguments of Badinter's, that is, that maternal love can be induced by capitalist interests, that we try to conclude a thought that you don't necessarily have to bear a child to love it.

This is what happens to Conceiçao when she adopts a child. By adopting, Conceiçao occupies a place socially assigned to mothers, and it is with a certain satisfaction that she concludes that: "- After all, I can also say that I raised a son..." (QUEIROZ, 2015, p. 162). In addition, based on Badinter's work, it is possible to affirm that the child is loved more intensely than those children to whom the anthropologist refers as children who, as soon as they are born, are handed over to a wet nurse and are seen by their biological mother four or five years later.

Thus, the author states that "maternal love is not a feeling inherent to the condition of womanhood, it is not a determinism, but something that is acquired" (BADINTER, 1980, p. 10). As can be seen today, love has been a product of social evolution since the beginning of the 19th century, since, as an examination of historical data shows, in the 17th and 18th centuries, the very concept of a mother's love for her children was different: children were usually handed over to nannies from an early age to raise them for a certain period of time. "In this way, like all human feelings, it varies according to the socio-economic fluctuations of history" (BADINTER, 1980, p. 02).

An important aspect that will strengthen Conceiçao's idea of breaking with the marriage institution is the opposite ways in which the characters Conceiçao and Vicente have been shaped by the narrator, which is already exposed in chapter one when the girl ponders what a strange couple they would be. In her reflections on the aloofness in which her possible husband would remain, the character imagines herself in the future, when she tries to share with her husband some impression received from some reading she has done, and reflects: "Perhaps Vicente would raise his eyes and murmur a distracted 'é' behind the newspaper..." (QUEIROZ, 2015, p. 88). In other words, the distance between the perspectives, the difference in habits between the two is something that bothers Conceiçao, a girl brought up in a family that was at odds with the family models that surrounded her in that era. These reflections lead her to realize how uncomfortable a possible union between the two would be.

After the novel **O Quinze** was published, the character Conceiçâo, in the way she was constructed by the narrator, became a reference for Rachel's other characters who would inherit the force of the rupture she inaugurated, which opened their eyes to the possibility of breaking free from the imprisoning system of patriarchy. It can be seen that the character becomes a reference, but she herself has no previous reference on which to base herself. It is up to her to start the process of breaking free from the shackles of tradition, as Bourdieu (2011) states.

On the other hand, Conceiçao had a prototypical faithful to this traditional system, her grandmother Dona Inacia. She, on the other hand, played the role of the patriarchal system in the work, with her censures that oppressed her granddaughter's sense of freedom in the face of her choice, even though she was twenty-two, not to talk about marriage. Her grandmother calmly told her that "a woman who doesn't marry is a cripple" (QUEIROZ, 2015. p.11), that Conceiçâo had "twisted her nature" (QUEIROZ, 2015. p.136), and also that her granddaughter's reading was "nonsense" (QUEIROZ, 2015. p. 136), thus reinforcing the patriarchal voice that echoed throughout society.

According to the philosopher Nietzche, the idea of a tradition instituted by God would prevent people from thinking about the possibility of questioning it in any way, reinforcing it for decades or centuries (NIETZCHE, [1895] / (2008), p.111). Dona Inàcia's statements illustrate exactly what the philosopher said, considering the degree of religiosity practiced by the woman. It is up to Conceiçao, then, to vehemently rebut these statements with force and decisiveness. To this end, she does so by reading Renan and Nordau, who help her to free herself from the patriarchal impositions of her grandmother, who, despite being a woman, often takes a stand in favor of this repressive tradition with which Conceiçao simply does not agree.

This is where we find one of Conceiçao's most important characteristics: wisdom, which she uses to keep herself free from this traditional fate. In a work that discusses happiness, the Brazilian psychiatrist, professor and writer Jorge Augusto Cury states the following: "An intelligent person learns from their mistakes, a wise person from the mistakes of others" (CURY, 2003, p. 30). Even though we know that Cury's (2003) phrase has become a buzzword, the next point provides an excellent opportunity to apply it. It cannot be categorically stated that there were indications in Conceiçao's family that showed negative aspects of marriage, in such a way as to make the girl choose to enjoy the freedom that her intellectual status afforded her.

It is known that the mother died early and there is no trace of any information about the father. It is also known that the grandmother is a widow, nor is there any mention of the grandfather, apart from his intellectual legacy and how he influenced Conceiçao with his library. What can be inferred from the period in which Conceiçao lived, the 1915s, and the space in which the narrative takes place, is that the character, despite living in an androcentric environment, had no male presence by her side throughout her upbringing. Conceiçâo was raised by her grandmother, the widow Dona Inàcia. As a result, she grew up with only female companionship and the intellectual legacy of her grandfather. In this context, she grew up independent of a physical male and paternal presence.

The environment in which she was brought up, then, did not allow her to experience a husband/wife relationship along the lines of the traditional family, which would allow her to form an opinion of what marriage was. In this way, the character compares her life and her model of family organization to other models and other feminine behaviours beyond her domestic environment, fulfilling in herself what Cury (2003) says about learning, that is, observing in the people around her the way marriage is socially conceived, not needing to position herself as the submissive and sad woman that Cordulina is in order to understand what it was like to be a traditional wife in the 1915s. Based on these assumptions, the narrator shows the same phenomenon in the 1930s, in other words, in her narrative she talks about women who break free from the bonds of tradition and live happily regardless of whether or not they get married.

It is not said that Conceiçao was averse to marriage. In fact, when the girl observes her cousin Vicente, the boy even awakens in her a faint desire to experience marriage. And it arouses her so much that we can see that, before concluding that the intellectual difference between her and Vicente becomes a difficult crossroads, the girl poetically compares him to beautiful aspects of nature:

> It now appeared to him as one of those corners of the forest, next to a stream, in a mysterious and comforting shade. Passing by on a hot midday, at the plodding trot of a horse, you stop there, look at the shade and the green as if you were going to a little corner of heaven... (QUEIROZ, 2015. p.88).

But the idea of getting married simply to fulfill a social role, in which women gave themselves to marriage just to tell society "I have a husband", didn't appeal to her.

In the character's poetic comparison, mentioned above, Vicente is compared to the relief that the corner of the forest near a stream would bring to someone who, passing through a hot midday sun, would feel refreshed. At the same time, when she wakes up, Conceiçao realizes that her cousin's rude way of dealing with life would be the midday sun that cancelled out the warm freshness of the woods. Thus, her thoughts turn to a more realistic comparison of her cousin's behavior, because it was also as if:

> Returning later, on a rainy morning, you find the sweet corner muddy, covered in worms, the beautiful trunks slippery and muddy, the surrounding branches dripping sadly. The first time, you think about spending your whole life in that freshness and peace; but the last time, you leave with a heavy heart, cured of bucolicism for a long time, sold on the reality of how aggressive and fickle nature is... (QUEIROZ, 2015. p. 88).

In this wise exercise of observation, her predictions are cold and rational; in fact, she knew that in the context in which she lived, a marriage dissolution was something reprehensible, if not impossible. And it is with great insight that the girl points out that:

> He was good to listen to and to look at, like a beautiful landscape, from which only beauty and color were required, but in times of storm, abandonment, or solitude, where would he look for the safe companion who understands and teaches, and completes the incomplete thought, and discusses the ideas that are coming,

and understands and responds to the inventions that the wandering mind creates? (QUEIROZ, 2015, p. 88).

Her mind was made up. Vicente didn't seem like the man she could be tied to for life, which allows her to conclude, along with her mother Nàcia, that "I've never found anyone worthwhile" (QUEIROZ, 2015, p.136). The reader is still unaware of this decision, but she already knows. The landscape would only be a visual delight. Nothing more.

Perhaps this was one of the main points that made her say this to her mother Nàcia. Conceiçao's words are direct, revealing and sincere. This is because, in constructing them, the narrator makes the reader very aware of who Conceiçao is. This awareness allows the reader to enter into the character's deepest reflections and one of the moments in which this reflection is perceived is precisely when she compares Vicente to this beautiful landscape, from which only beauty and color are required. Thus, in the work of narrative construction, we see that Rachel de Queiroz accomplishes what was said by Beth Brait (1985) when analyzing the construction of the character, when she states that:

Like a sorcerer who mixes potions in a magical cauldron, the writer resorts to the artifices offered by a code in order to create his creatures. Whether they are taken from his real or imaginary experience, from dreams, nightmares or the pettiness of everyday life, the materiality of these beings can only be achieved through a game of language that makes their presence tangible and their movements sensitive (BRAIT, 1985, p. 52).

In fact, it is through the narrator's omniscience that the reader will enter the consciousness of the character Conceiçao and realize how critically the girl views the foundations of the patriarchal society in which she lives, from which her break with tradition will make her an emblematic character in the history of Brazilian literature. After all, Conceiçao breaks with tradition without any identity crisis, since she remains a woman, happy and a mother.

When it comes to female identity, an important name to evoke is that of Betty Friedan. In her work, The **Feminine Mystique**, published in 1963, the women's activist deals with women's conflict in the face of the wave of consumerism that grew stronger every year in the United States. Although her work is *a priori* aimed at American society, the writer Rose Marie Muraro, a Brazilian intellectual and feminist who has written more than forty books, states when introducing Friedan's work that:

Friedan's denunciation doesn't just apply to the United States. With the usual lag, Brazilian society is also approaching the highest standards of consumption, especially in the big cities. The problem she raises also begins to be the problem of urban Brazilian women (FRIEDAN, 1963, p. 07).

We therefore agree with Rose Marie when she suggests that Brazilian women live between two major vicissitudes: expanding a professional career or dedicating themselves to training and caring for their families, spending their time between husband and children. Friedan's work is important and liberating for many women in the 20th century. Friedan reveals that many women, including herself, upon graduating or achieving their professional dream, were faced with a simple and conflicting question: "Is this really what I want?" (FRIEDAN, 1963, p. 62).

In contrasting Friedan and Badinter, Elisabeth Badinter's work shows how capitalism was responsible for the formation of a period in which the only behavior expected of women was submission to marriage. In 1963, Betty Friedan preceded reflection on this issue by using empirical experiments to show the complexity of being a woman and highlighting the great conflict experienced by the female subject between the freedom to be who one wants to be and the social constraints of the "woman of the home" so cruelly ignored. Many women observed in the interviews and studies carried out by the researcher were faced with this conflict. Friedan starts by describing her own dilemma, as can be seen in the fragment below:

> I remember a quiet spring afternoon on the Smith *campus* in 1942 when I came to a frightening impasse about my future. A few days earlier, I had received news that I had been awarded a postgraduate scholarship. While I was receiving congratulations, I felt, underneath my excitement, a strange uncertainty, a questioning that I didn't want to think about [...]. I couldn't go back. I couldn't go back home, to the life of my mother and the women of our town, tied to the home, the bridge, the shopping, the children, the husband, the clothes, the charity work. But now that the time had come to realize my future, to take the decisive step, I suddenly didn't know what to do (FRIEDAN, 1963, p. 62).

In her search for an answer that would make her feel more comfortable, the one that most reassured her was the one she got from a doctor's wife, a mother of three, who had been out of university for fifteen years. The woman, drinking coffee in the kitchen of her New England home, made the following statement:

> The tragedy is that no one has ever looked us in the face and said: "You need to sort out what you want out of your life, apart from being a wife and mother". I never thought about it until I was thirty-six. [...] I always thought, as a child, that when I grew up I would go to university and then get married. For me, this was the culmination of a girl's desires. [...] It wasn't until, as a doctor's wife, I felt so lonely and started shouting at the children because they wouldn't let me be happy, that I realized I needed personal interests. I hadn't yet decided what my life would be. I hadn't finished evolving (FRIEDAN, 1963, p. 64).

We can see that this wife's liberation didn't come about by forcing herself to do the course or by refraining from doing it because of her husband and children. It happened when she realized that one thing doesn't necessarily cancel out the other, that she could, if she decided, and that's what she decided and freed her, as well as being a wife and mother, attend a course, reconciling her objectives. This is what she was referring to in her conversation with Friedan, and what no one had warned her about. No one confronted women and showed them these possibilities. Thus, it can be understood that there are at least three possibilities for a woman: to be a wife, a mother and to cultivate a personal dream within herself. It can be seen that one alternative does not exclude the other and it is up to the woman to decide which she chooses.

The first possibility is to be a wife and mother only, putting aside the possible dream of going to university; the other possibility is to be a wife and mother (without having a husband) and reconciling these two jobs with the personal dream of going to university; or, as a priority, to go to university while giving up the role of wife and mother. What's more, there's nothing to stop a woman from prioritizing her dream of going to university and then thinking about marriage and motherhood, which is what the protagonist of the novel in question has opted for. Conceiçao already appears in the novel as a graduate, working as a teacher without any conflict either with her profession or with her single life. Even with this certainty, she still thinks about the possibility of marriage to her cousin, which doesn't materialize. However, she becomes a mother, adopting a child, and in this way dispels any idea that her choice would make her unhappy, like the women analyzed by Friedan.

4 WOMEN'S WRITING IN THE FIFTEEN

We always know something about our parents, a fact, a distinction. They were soldiers or sailors; they held such a position or made such a law. But what remains of our mothers, grandmothers and great-grandmothers? Nothing but a tradition. One was beautiful; another had red hair; a third was kissed by the queen. We know nothing about them except their names, the dates of their marriages and the number of children they had (WOOLF, 2014, p.170).

When trying to define or categorize, in a more formal way, what women's writing is or means, it is possible to arrive at more than one answer or none at all. It is not clear to the layman whether women's writing is writing about women, for women or produced by women. The words of the Mozambican writer Mia Couto, author of several works whose writing is considered "feminine", corroborate these uncertainties when, in an interview with Rita de Càssia Natal Chaves in Belo Horizonte, he says that at the beginning of his career, when he was announced for a lecture or interview in a certain city or country, the audience expected to see a woman writer in front of them: "I confess it's been easier now, but at first there were countries where I arrived and they were expecting someone else. A black woman. It was difficult to explain that it was me." (COUTO, 2017).

Throughout this chapter, it will be possible to understand more clearly what, apart from the name, made the writer be mistaken for a woman. It's not a question of analyzing the femininity or otherwise of a name, but rather the profile through which his writing passes. At another time when violence against women was being discussed, Couto states that: "One of the reasons for this violence against women, I think, is fear. Men are afraid of this, of what a woman can be for them. He's afraid when the woman is silent, he's afraid when the woman speaks. Because he has a profound lack of knowledge about her" (COUTO, 2017).

In the light of the above, the issue of women's writing will initially be addressed in the light of Lucia Castelo Branco's reflections. The scholar admits that something relating to women happens out there, although this relating to women, she says, cannot be understood as something produced by them (BRANCO, 1991, p.12). One can thus see the great responsibility one has when one simply utters the expression "women's writing" and doesn't even think about the complexity of the term.

In fact, there is a tendency to assign a genre to writing or even to literature itself. Constância Lima Duarte states that:

In the field of literature, one of the most debated questions continues to be whether or not there is a specific form of women's literature. Already the subject of a number of articles and essays among us, the issue crosses borders and has become the subject of seminars and various works, which contribute to further increasing the discussion. With regard to literary themes and genres, they are unanimous in pointing to some that would be more "suitable" for women, such as sentimental novels and those of psychological confession, "such is female sensitivity" (DUARTE, 1987, p. 17, emphasis added).

And it is this very "feminine sensibility" that will lead us to reflect, throughout this chapter, on what "women's writing" is. Duarte (1987) discusses the great interest among theorists and scholars in studies and research on women, emphasizing the results of research on feminism in the 1960s and 1970s. And such research was obviously not done without considering what had been produced in the literature. It is a notorious fact, as Duarte (1987) also observes, that there is a great mark that runs through all literary texts produced by men, which seek to reinforce a stereotype of behavior that is expected of women. She points out that "If we carefully re-read some of the works of our literature, observing the images of women constructed therein, we can see how they are loaded with stereotypes derived from the patriarchal society established here". (DUARTE, 1987), in other words, male writing produced the female stereotype according to its own interests.

Both Simone de Beauvoir and Constância Lima Duarte discuss issues related to feminism in a context between the 1950s and 1980s, which Rachel de Queiroz had already anticipated in the 1930s in her novel **O Quinze**. With Conceiçâo, the author has already presented a form of break with tradition that the philosopher and the researcher mentioned above will discuss in the future. When Conceiçâo, for example, reads a work that "deals with women's issues, the situation of women in society, maternal rights, etc" (QUEIROZ, 2015. p. 135), she questions all the patriarchal impositions to which women are subjected.

Another characteristic that is considered important in women's writing, also observed by Constância Lima Duarte (1987), is the way in which many male characters are constructed, devoid of the grandeur typical of literature written by men. In the literature produced by women, this grandeur is not so common. Duarte observes that

> There is also frequent astonishment at the representation of the male figure in certain texts by women, which are very different from the stereotype of the virile, strong and superior man found in texts by men. Màrio de Andrade went so far as to accuse Raquel de Queiróz of "vengeful weakness in analyzing men" and "revenge of the eternal masculine" (DUARTE, 1987, p. 20, emphasis added).

In parallel with Mario de Andrade's statement, Rachel de Queiroz's writing already anticipates what Duarte (1987) says, when she builds the profile of the character Vicente in a way that falls short of the expectations of the character Conceiçao. Vicente boasts pompously when he says that all he understood about books was the cattle note (QUEIROZ, 2015, p. 14), which doesn't sound at all positive according to patriarchal values. In the narrative, the idea of smallness, conveyed by Vicente's mother when she ponders her son, demonstrates this "vengeful weakness" that Duarte (1987) comments that Mârio de Andrade denounces. An example of this is when the narrator presents the scene of a party to inaugurate a gramophone at the Major's house, where:

> Vicente's mother, sitting on the sofa enjoying the dance, saw only the depressing contrast between her son's rudeness and the practicality of the others, with their tousled hair, elegant creased pants and thin shirts under their homemade blouses, on her end of the sofa, the poor lady felt her eyes fill with tears, and she stayed there crying for her son, so handsome, so strong, who wasn't ashamed of the difference he made from his brother, the doctor, and insisted on not wanting to "be people" (QUEIROZ, 2015, p. 20, emphasis added). 20, emphasis added).

Thus, while Conceiçao is presented as a woman ahead of her time, an example for the next Queirosean characters who break with the traditional paradigm that imposed on women a marriage governed by the oppressive patriarchal system until then, Vicente is, at some point, presented as a figure ridiculed and stereotyped by the customs of the sertâo and the ignorance of a cattle caretaker.

4.1 Women's writing (?)

A key characteristic when analyzing women's writing, as opposed to men's, is the literary tone, which has been worked on by some theorists, including Alfredo Bosi. According to Bosi, "there is no great artistic text that has not been generated within a dialectic of pure memory and social memory" (BOSI, 1988, p. 278). Bosi's arguments meet dialogically with Octavio Paz's statement that "no text is completely original, because language itself, in its essence, is already a translation: firstly, of the non-verbal world and, secondly, because every sign and every sentence is the translation of another sign and another sentence" (PAZ, 1971 *apud* ARROJO, 2007, p. 11).

Bosi explains that what mediates the dialog between one sign and another are the literary perspective and tone. According to the author, "perspective and tone are the mediating concepts of this mediation par excellence" (BOSI, 1988, p. 278). Understanding what this literary tone means becomes *a sine qua non* condition for pursuing studies of women's writing, a perspective that is in line with the approaches of Lucia Castelo Branco and Sunday Adetunji, as will be seen below. According to Bosi's studies, it can be seen that:

> In literature, the term tone [...] refers to the affective modalities of expression. [...] The classifications of literary genres and subgenres are based on tone. Pathetic tone, elegiac tone, satirical tone, famous tone, festive tone, idyllic tone, heroic tone, epic tone, serious tone, burlesque tone, sapiential tone, ironic tone, etc. (BOSI, 1988, p. 279).

Thus, much more than simply being written by women, the texts considered to be women's writing carry their own tone and, peculiarly, are literarily recognized as such. After analyzing numerous texts written by women, Lucia Castelo Branco began to weave her investigative web, noticing a peculiarity common to several texts written by women. The researcher realizes that these texts distinguish themselves from others and resemble each other "because they have a tone, a diction, a rhythm, a breath of their own" (BRANCO, 1991, p.13). However, lay readers are mistaken in thinking that these characteristics are only possible in writings by women, as she explains: "by referring to tone, diction, breathing, I mean that something other than the themes chosen by these women ended up distinguishing their writing" (BRANCO, 1991, p.14). The author finishes this reasoning by explaining the issue of writing she considers to be feminine, but done by the hands of men, as shown in the following excerpt:

> But what interested me, right from the start, was not so much the depths of the texts produced by women, but their surface: the inflection of the voice, the breath that is usually both slow and hasty, the oralizing tone of their writing. And these characteristics - I would soon admit - were not restricted to texts produced by women: Marcel Proust also possessed this enunciation, some Guimarães Rosa at certain moments "spoke" in this diction and even James Joyce, when completely taken over by the magic and excess of language, made himself heard in this way, femininely (BRANCO, 1991, p. 14).

It's clear that the author wants to demystify the idea that women's writing is only that produced by women, although, for her, a large number of these writings are produced by women. But the tone to which Branco refers is charged with a "caress that the sound, the rhythm, the modulation of the voice and the breath can produce in the reader's ear, like a light breath in a baby's ear" (BRANCO, 1991, p. 50). This feminine tone can be perceived in some excerpts from Rachel de Queiroz's work, as shown in the following excerpt:

> Cordulina began to cry again; Chico Bento himself quickly wiped his sleeve across his face. Rendeira stared into all of his big, painful eyes, from which a clear stripe ran down his dark muzzle like a trail of tears. Only Mocinha looked at the reindeer with indifference, fixed her slippers in her hand and continued walking with her soft step, so fast and light that it barely crushed the brittle clods on the ground (QUEIROZ, 2015, p. 42).

As the family leaves the serão, they are surprised by the tearful gaze of a reindeer called Rendeira, who for so many years had served them with her work and breastfeeding the children, and who now, there in the caustic serão, was coming closer and closer to death. Even though she is referring here to a relationship between the family and the animal, commonly seen as a being devoid of emotion, the narrator does so in a different way. The tone of sadness imprinted in each of the words reinforces a feeling that humanizes the animal and the melancholy felt by the reader is the same as that observed in a situation of abandonment of a human being, as if the family were abandoning a loved one:

> She listened, weeping, wiping her tear-blinded eyes on the hammock's red balcony. The slow, tired voice vibrated, rose, sounded different, embracing projects and ambitions. And the hopeful imagination smoothed out the difficult roads, forgot longing, hunger and anguish, penetrated the green shade of the Amazon,

> overcame brute nature, dominated the beasts and the visages, made him rich and victorious. Cordulina listened, and opened her heart to that hope; but as she ran her eyes along the rammed earth walls, to the corner where her little son slept in the patched hammock, she again felt a pang of longing, and regretted it (QUEIROZ, 2015, p. 32).

The tone of anguish, intermingled with the green of the Amazon, which would suggest hope, gives the scene the sensation of a breath being produced in the reader's ear, like a light breath in a baby's ear, as Lùcia Castelo Branco puts it (BRANCO, 1991, p.50). And these subtle characteristics present in this type of writing can be found in works written by women as well as men, as is the case with Mia Couto and some of the authors cited by the scholar, such as Guimarâes Rosa, James Joyce, Marcel Proust, etc.

When we consider the passages quoted from Rachel de Queiroz, which are capable of allowing her to be identified as a woman's writer, we come across the delicate comment by Graciliano Ramos, quoted in Chapter One, who, on reading Queiroz's first novel, questions its authorship, suggesting that her name could be the pseudonym of a bearded man. Ramos does not perceive this subtlety, this "caressing tone" in Queiroz's writing, and wonders if it was really a woman's writing. The author thus reinforces the internalized prejudice of the patriarchal voice, making clear the reduced space given to women in the literary field, which until then had been exclusive to men.

Nevertheless, Queiroz went beyond the simple publication of a novel, being the first woman to occupy, as already mentioned, chair number five of the Brazilian Academy of Letters, taking office on November 4, 1977, wearing her imposing uniform, until then reserved only for men.

4.2 Creating your own writing environment

This topic deals primarily with aspects of women's writing in general, and only then will there be a specific approach to Rachel de Queiroz's writing. However, some consideration will be given to the construction of the character Conceiçao, given her great importance in the work. An important starting point, for example, is how much reading and types of reading influence her, shaping her entire construction. Conceiçao appears to be linked not only to literary readings, such as Sienkiewicz's novel, but also to philosophical and social readings.

to social issues, such as Max Nordau and Ernest Renan:

> He grabbed the first book his hand could reach, made a pile of pillows in the corner of the bed, near the light, and, leaning his elbow on them, opened the volume wide. It was an old Polish story, a novel by Sienkiewicz, recounting cases of heroism, rebellion and guerrilla warfare (QUEIROZ, 2015, p. 10).

Although the character was indeed fascinated by novels like Sienkiewicz's, his interest in reading and discussing philosophers like the two mentioned is explicit. We see one of his reflections, for example, when he replies to his mother Nàcia that the work he was reading was about "serious matters" (QUEIROZ, 2015, p. 135). Although she holds her grandmother in high esteem, her thoughts lead to at least one other reflection that is no less important: the scene in which Conceiçao tries to draw Dona Inacia's attention to the seriousness of her reading. Arguing that her reading is a "serious matter", before returning to her, she makes the following reflection: "[...] in order to avoid excessive helplessness, people need to create their environment, their ideas, their reforms, their apostolate... although they may never do it... or even try... but at least project them, and mentally build them up..." (QUEIROZ, 2015, p. 10).

In Conceiçao's reflections, we can see the possibility of a discussion between what the character learned from her reading and the thinking of one of the greatest writers and feminists of the late 19th century, Virginia Woolf, when she discusses women's space in her work **A Roof All Your Own,** published in 1929. By defending the need for physical space for women as fundamental for them to be able to write, Woolf metaphorizes a discussion about women's space in society as a whole, considering space in more than one of its conceptions.

We note that her discussion touches on the problem of the representation of women in and through writing. Still from Woolf's work, the writer addresses the question of a woman's need to create her own space, her own environment, which enables her to write her own fiction. The woman, she says, needs to create a financial independence that allows her to write, that gives her more freedom and allows her to feel independent of patriarchal ties. At the beginning of her work, the author states:

> All I could do was offer you an opinion on one insignificant aspect: a woman needs to have money and a roof over her head if she really wants to write fiction; and that, as you will see, leaves the great problem of the true nature of woman and the true nature of fiction unsolved. I have shirked the duty of reaching a conclusion on these two questions - woman and fiction, as far as I am concerned, remain unsolved problems (WOOLF, 1985, p. 08).

Before going into the question of representation itself, it is necessary to mention another name, in addition to Lucia Castelo Branco's, to provide a more solid basis for the discussion on women's writing. That name is Sunday Adetunji Bamisile, a scholar who combines writing and women's space in his reflections, a subject dealt with by Virginia Woolf. A priori, Bamisile states that:

> When women assumed that literary writing was also their space, this meant a revolution in the socio-cultural and psychological sphere of women, first and foremost, and to a certain extent also an intrusion into a space

of cultural expression that had previously always been dominated by men (BAMISILE, 2012, p. 39).

Bamisile thus corroborates Branco's words when he attests to the disconnection of women's writing from the female sex. According to him, women's writing has developed through three distinct phases, one of which is of direct interest to this study, in which the work under analysis is included. This is the third phase, which covers the period from 1920 to the present day. Since **O Quinze** appears in 1930, it can be classified as a work from the third phase advocated by Bamisile. According to the scholar, this phase is configured as:

The phase of women's greatest confrontation with the stronghold of patriarchal values. This long-standing moment witnessed a lively awareness among women of their rights and was given a crucial boost from the 1960s onwards, when the patriarchal edifice was challenged by other protests (BAMISILE, 2012, p. 44).

In the light of Bamisile's considerations, the character Conceiçao finds herself in exactly this context of confrontation, breaking with an age-old tradition of patriarchal values. Without caring about the external dictates, the accusations coming mainly from the patriarchal voice of Dona Inacia, the girl assumes her role as a representative of women, fulfilling what Bamisile points out when he says that "the female character can be considered to be the (I) that represents women" (BAMISILE, 2012, p. 44).

4.3 The representation of women by women

When talking about representation, it is important to delimit and clarify what is being called representation. In philosophy, representation is understood as "something that stands for something else. There is one thing: the representative, which stands for something else, the represented. Thus, representation is a relationship between the representative and the represented" (BOLNOIS, 1999, p. 26, apud GAMBARATO, 2005, p. 207). When it comes to the representation of the feminine in works written by men, it is possible to recognize that this representation may be open to question. This is what Bamisile suggests when working with African literature, in a reflection that can be extended to other literatures. In his reflection on the relationship between women's writing and representation, the theorist states that:

In African literature, the representation of female characters by male novelists shows a tendency to be oriented towards a male audience, insisting on stereotypes that diminish women. [...] And any attempt to present a contrary idea is seen by them as an obvious deviation from the tradition where women are relegated to the background, as docile and unimportant characters (BAMISILE, 2012, p. 67).

The author goes on to show that there is a change in this perspective from the moment when there is a more effective participation of women in literature. Bamisile's approach, i.e. a denouncing approach, sees the representation of women in literature as being completely tainted by patriarchal sentiment.

Another aspect to be considered when it comes to representation is the reflection of Antônio Cândido, who emphasizes the issue of literature as social representation when he analyses the work **Senhora**, by José de Alencar. When talking about Aurélia's marriage and referring to the dowry that the girl pays to her fiancé, Cândido states that "this purchase has a symbolic social meaning, since it is both a representation and an unmasking of customs in force at the time, such as marriage for money" (CÂNDIDO, 2000, p. 7).

Although the intention of the work is to critically discuss capitalism and the practice of dowry, the narrator does not fail to convey a tone of degeneration when developing the profile of the female character Aurélia. In many scenes we see a woman who is sarcastic, ironic, cold, indifferent and proud of the power that money has given her. When you analyze some other female characters in Brazilian literature who were delineated by the vision of patriarchal pity, you discover how most of them follow a certain archetype of slave-like submission, if not creatures who were clearly degenerated by the narrator, being built from a clearly negative stereotype.

Examples include Rita baiana in **O Cortiço** (1981), Magdà in **O homem** (1887) and Amélia in **Casa** de **Pensao** (2013), all by Aluizio de Azevedo. This type of problem regarding the (non-)representation of women is also discussed in **Gender and Representation in Brazilian Literature** (2002), organized by Constância Lima Duarte, Eduardo de Assis Duarte and Kâtia da Costa Bezerra. In the text **A mulher na Literatura: gênero e representaçao (Women in Literature: Gender and Representation**), Lia Scholze, in the wake of Michel Foucault, when working on the question of the discursive strategies present in these works developed under the patriarchal system of writing, states that:

> Throughout history, women have suffered a process of silencing and exclusion. The subject who speaks is always male in literature, in law and in the courtroom. They are reserved the places of prominence, making men more visible. [...] The failure of women is therefore present in the discourses that build up expectations of women as those responsible for looking after the family and the home. Her duties are to procreate, manage the house, the food and the movements of the family members. The characters' frustrations are linked to their failure to fulfill these roles successfully (SCHOLZE, 2002, p.174-182).

However, as we are talking about women's writing (and not writing about women), it is necessary to try to break out of this framework that makes women be seen through the manipulative lens of men's writing.

Another important distinction to be made is the distance between women's writing and feminism. To this end, it is important to look here at one of the writers who has focused her attention on this issue of the feminine and feminism: Simone Beauvoir. In her work **The Second Sex - Facts and Myths** (1970), the philosopher begins by stating the following:

"León Richier was the true founder of feminism, creating *Les Droits de la Femme* and organizing the international congress on these rights in 1878" (BEAUVOIR, 1970, p. 158).

Women's suffrage is undoubtedly the starting point that led thousands of women and a few men to begin this real war for emancipation

women. Over the years, it has become clear that, although it is a great achievement, the right to vote alone is too little in the face of women's desire, capacity and strength. Beauvoir argues how hard it was for women to achieve a certain visibility. From León Richier's congress in 1878 to the present day, many uprisings, demonstrations, hunger strikes, confrontations and thousands of deaths had to take place for women to achieve the condition of being and having what they have and are today. The quest to establish women's rights took place simultaneously in several countries. Before Leon Richier's congress, Miss Anthony, a great feminist leader, founded the National Association for the Suffrage of Women in 1869. According to Beauvoir:

> That same year, the state of Wyoming granted women the right to vote. But it wasn't until 1893 that Colorado and then, in 1896, Idaho and Utah followed suit. [...] In 1900, there were 5 million women working in the United States, 1,300,000 of them in industry, 500,000 in commerce; a good number of them were in commercial and industrial enterprises, in business and in the liberal professions. There are lawyers, doctors and 3,373 women pastors. The famous Mary Baker Eddy founded the *Christian Scientist Church.* Women are accustomed to meeting in clubs, which in 1900 had around two million members (BEAUVOIR, 1970, p. 163).

When you look back at the bloody years of struggle for women's emancipation, you can get an idea of the many hidden motives in the patriarchal mind, which fought as long as it could to embargo women's rights out of fear that women might emerge from their subordinate condition.

This fear led to many absurdities being spoken and written about, as in the case of Rousseau, who went so far as to say that "All the education of women must be relative to men.... Woman is made to yield to man and bear his injustices" (ROUSSEAU *apud* BEAUVOIR, 1970, p. 140). In the same vein, Pierre Proudhon, a French philosopher, politician and economist, stated in his work entitled **La justice** that:

> [...] woman must remain dependent on man; only he is of value as a social individual; there is no association in the couple, which would presuppose equality, but a union; woman is inferior to man, firstly because her physical strength is only two thirds of his, then because she is intellectually and morally inferior to him in the same proportion: her value is 2x2x2 as opposed to 3x3x3, i.e. 8/27 of that of the stronger sex (PROUDHON *apud* BEAUVOIR, 1970, p. 147). 147).

The statements made by these thinkers have, of course, caused a stir. However, they allow us to understand the level of fear that exists within the patriarchy in the face of female emancipation, which is becoming increasingly visible. Finally, on the struggle of women in the first quarter of the 20th century, Beauvoir says:

In 1917, a few days before the revolution, on the occasion of International Women's Day on March 8, they held a large demonstration in the streets of St. Petersburg, demanding bread, peace and the return of their husbands. They took part in the October uprising; between 1918 and 1920 they played a major economic and even military role in the fight against the invaders. True to the Marxist tradition, Lenin linked the emancipation of women to that of the workers; he gave them political equality and economic equality (BEAUVOIR, 1970, p. 165).

Lenin's intention to grant this political and economic equality to women is clear, since by appearing generous to the working class and women, his popularity would tend to grow. Once again, patriarchy is directing women's destiny under the guise of doing good. In fact, this is what we see in Elizabeth Badinter's work when she argues about the constant hand of patriarchy in inducing maternal love.

All this research carried out by Beauvoir shows how slow women's emancipation was and still is, beginning with the fight for the right to suffrage and extending to other areas. Literature contributes a lot to this process by creating female characters who express the demands of women, as Bamisile shows us when she states that:

Women's literary production that seeks to give greater expression to the worldview of women in the world and to raise awareness of the cause of women naturally gives prominence to female characters who convey their own desires and affirm their questions in the face of this same world, which has not yet given them the right space for representation. Highlighting the role of these characters will also help us to emphasize the way in which African-American literary production has become a voice denouncing the excesses of patriarchal systems in relation to women, all over the world (BAMISILE, 2012, p. 61).

Bamisile's considerations are in line with what we have tried to propose throughout this work when analyzing the Queirosean character Conceiçao, who, in Brazilian literature, represents a break with the patriarchal tradition of marriage. By inaugurating this break, Conceiçâo gives prominence to the next Queirosean characters who succeed her in the role of assuming a "voice of denunciation of the excesses of patriarchal systems towards women" (BAMISILE, 2012, p. 61).

In this way, Raquel de Queiroz's writing fulfills a social role through the performance of the character Conceiçao, insofar as it makes it possible to discuss both writing and the representation of women.

4.4 Rachel de Queiroz, feminist?

Although some theorists insist on claiming that Rachel de Queiroz was a feminist, the author insisted on saying that she had never been one and that it had never been her intention to raise any kind of banner for or against, leaving some theorists suspicious of such a stance, thinking it was just an act. In an interview with TV Cultura's **Roda Viva** program in 1991, Rachel categorically defended her non-adherence to feminism. Below is an excerpt from the interview, in which journalist Fàbio Lucas, using the statements of a feminist scholar in São Paulo, says that Rachel's feminism is very patriarchal, to which she replies:

Rachel de Queiroz: But I've never been a feminist. I was never a feminist in the first place.

Fàbio Lucas: That's exactly why.

Rachel de Queiroz: I'm not a feminist. I think society has to grow together. The association between women and men is very good and I think it's a big mistake to fight against men. That joke we say, "that man was made to serve woman"... It really was [laughs], so I've never been a feminist, I've always disagreed with feminists. And since I think that the human condition is one of suffering and disappointment and that age only brings bitterness and renunciation and conformism, then my women, like my men too... Except that I dedicate myself more to women's stories, in fact, my main characters are always women.[7]

Although Rachel considers herself a non-feminist, her works are currently adopted as sources for various studies in this area. Regardless of whether or not the author considers herself a feminist, it is believed that her work is fundamental to the construction of female identity in Brazilian literature. As has already been said, the revolutionary advance of women's intellectual development became clear in the 1930s, and it became extremely important to take something that belonged only to men out of male control: the mastery of writing. And as Constância Lima Duarte states:

The constitution of female identity, thus considered and formulated by men, was completely riddled with prejudices and ideologies. That's why it was necessary to wait for women to take the floor, impose themselves in the public arena and finally build their own representations (DUARTE, 2009, p. 31).

And this certainly happened in 1930 with Rachel de Queiroz, who proposed a new vision of women *in* her novel **O Quinze**. Based on this new model of representation created in the work, women can see themselves as the directors of their own destiny, occupying places that were once impossible for them, as was the case with the writer at the Brazilian Academy of Letters in 1977. If in non-fictional life, women take on certain spaces not previously occupied by women, fictional life will only reproduce them, which is one of the roles of literature, as portrayed in **O Quinze**, in which a girl builds her own destiny amid criticism and accusations that her refusal to marry would make her "a cripple" (QUEIROZ, 2015, p.11). Such was the importance of the novel in 1930 that Duarte adds of Rachel de Queiroz's work that:

7 As the information is taken from electronic media, it *is* not possible to indicate the page.

The narrator thus renews the cycle of drought, but mainly renews the representation of women, because from her perspective she creates characters who cease to be objects and finally become subjects of the narrative (DUARTE, 2009, p. 31).

In other words, with regard to the work being part of the drought cycle, Raquel de Queiroz and her work **O Quinze** present a new way of inserting women, not those who attracted all the patriarchal impositions to themselves, nor those who sought to invest in a marriage on the basis of a good dowry. Conceiçao goes far beyond this feminine bias and represents, as already mentioned, not only the break with an oppressive tradition of marriage, but also the struggle in favor of others by turning to those suffering from the drought. Fulfilling what Duarte (2009) says, the character stops being an object and becomes the subject of the narrative.

4.5 The decline of patriarchy

To consider the 1930s as the decade of the decline of patriarchy would be a real claim on our part. Therefore, it is necessary to delimit what was happening in practice with the patriarchal system in this period, which allows us to think of this decade at least as a driver of this decadence. It is already known that women acquired a great deal of knowledge and intellectual interest. To support this part of the study, we used the theory developed by Gilberto Freyre, a sociologist, historian and essayist of the 1900s and his work **Sobrados e mucambos** (1961), which works in detail on each stage of this decadence and the parallel rise of women at the time.

The anguish in which women lived at the beginning of the 20th century, due to a sense of abandonment caused by the great neglect of men who, accustomed to the powers acquired through the patriarchal system, felt increasingly superior to women, meant that they sought out the priest's confessional more and more often. Added to this was the large number of priests who graduated young, virile and ready to listen without sparing any time to women who didn't even have a voice at home, let alone in society. This can be attributed to the countless adulteries committed by young priests during this period, since the church was one of the few places where women were allowed to attend, and even then accompanied by their parents, as Eni de Mesquita Samara (1995, p. 64) tells us:

One of the most common stereotypes about Brazilian women in the past was their confinement and seclusion. Thus, women had little to do apart from obeying their husbands and looking after the house and children. According to historiography, they also had few opportunities for social life and, on the rare occasions when they did go out, it was to go to church on Sundays or to attend religious festivals, logically always accompanied by their father or husband. They therefore lived in the so-called permitted spaces and were obedient and submissive (SAMARA, 1995, p. 64).

Thus, as a result of the distressing confinement that caused the emptiness of loneliness in the family to grow more and more, the number of women who turned to the parish priest to vent their misfortunes and inner conflicts grew every day, as Freyre states:

> Moreover, in view of certain less controversial generalizations in psychoanalysis, in patriarchal societies where there is extreme seclusion or oppression of women, the confessional can be attributed a very useful function of hygiene, or rather mental sanitation. Through it, a lot of longing, a lot of repressed desire, which would otherwise fester inside the oppressed and repressed person, would have been drained away in the form of sin. By going to confession, they would detoxify themselves. They purged themselves. It was a cleansing for the nerves, and not just for their souls, anxious for heaven, where their little angel children were waiting for them, shouting "mamâe! mamâe!" (FREYRE, 1961, p. 94, emphasis added).

Another important fact is that, with the advance of science, the priest was gradually replaced by the figure of the doctor. There were obvious cases in which psychic pathologies, as soon as they caused a reaction in the body, resulted in a request for the doctor's presence as urgently as possible and in many cases what the doctor heard was that the young maiden really needed a good marriage to cure her spirits. And the patriarchy didn't notice that its arrogance was gradually crumbling and its decline was becoming clearer and clearer.

It was thanks to this "cleansing", this outflow that began in the confessionals and extended to the doctors' offices, that we can see that even in the midst of so much enclosure, in the midst of all the care taken to keep women submissive under the patriarchal clutches, we see the emergence of what Gilberto Freyre, as well as other theorists, called "the matriarchs". Women who were true mainstays on the farms, who, when they became widowed, for example, took over the business that had previously been their husbands' and did it as well as, or better than, their husbands. Gilberto Freyre mentions them in his work **Sobrados e mucambos**, pointing out that:

> Throughout the patriarchal era, there were women, especially plantation owners, in whom a greater social and not simply domestic energy exploded than that of ordinary men. Energy to manage farms, like the Joaquinas do Pompeu; energy to direct the family's party politics throughout a region, like the Franciscas do Rio Formoso; warrior energy, like that of the Pernambuco matrons who distinguished themselves during the war against the Dutch, not only in the two marches, to Alagoas and Bahia, through the woods and across deep rivers, but also at Tejucupapo, where it is traditional that they fought bravely against the heretics (FREYRE, 1961, p. 95).95).

The point is that from the end of the 19th century, these female figures were already showing signs of what was expected in the middle of the 20th century, extending into the 21st. These signs were clearly facilitated by the press and its role, given the proportions of the time. It is undeniable that the 1930s presented a picture of conflicting tensions in the relationship between men and women, both inside and outside of marriage. Maria de Fâtima Salum points out that:

With nuances and differentiations in relation to the way of thinking about male and female roles in social life and the relationship between the sexes, various voices repeatedly put women and marriage under suspicion. The numerous manifestations on these issues were presented in this press in the form of poetry, chronicles, jokes, caricatures, proverbs, etc. (SALUM, p. 26, 1997).

According to Salum (1997), one of the biggest vehicles for spreading and stimulating these tensions was the famous newspaper **Apito**, which in the early 1930s exerted a great influence on these tensions and on changing female behavior, either through criticism, irony or even indiscriminate disdain for women. In January 1932, the newspaper inaugurated the "Young Women's Section", where its editor answered letters from female readers who consulted him about sentimental problems. His advice, however, stopped at the level of debauchery, disdain and belittling of women. It is clear, however, to the eye of a more attentive observer, that the patriarchy is concerned about the rise of women and is therefore encouraging this type of predatory dissemination with all its might.

In addition to these internal influences, at the beginning of the second half of the 19th century there was a widespread French influence, showing concern about the emergence of a class that threatened the patriarchy. The new French fashions were evidently major influencers in this period, and it was impossible for them to go unnoticed. Thus, another aspect of this change began to emerge alongside the external conflicts. There was a preoccupation with studies that sought to demonstrate how much the body speaks by externalizing what one is inside. This is what happens with a woman's new relationship with her body. It is impossible for women of this period to remain with the same outward expression in the face of such a great inner transformation. All of this was influenced by the new European fashions, as can be seen below:

With the generalization of the more refined bourgeois European fashions and the urbanization of the once rustically patriarchal lifestyles, the deficiencies or excesses of body shapes that didn't correspond to the Paris and London fashions were corrected by means of ointments, cosmetics, false teeth and hair, hips, hair dyes and corsets. Corsets of which, from the first half of the 19th century, numerous advertisements appeared in Brazilian newspapers (FREYRE, 1961, p. 104).

This period saw the great influence of cosmetology products to help this new woman get as close as possible to the French model of beauty. It was no longer parents or the church who dictated the rules for women, but rather, paradoxically to the great process of female emancipation, the European model of how to conduct oneself in society. In the meantime, patriarchalism was gradually declining in Brazil and would never be the same again. The appeals were really tempting. Any woman who was distressed at being trapped under the cruel yoke of the Family, the State and the Church (the main apparatuses of domination studied by Louis Althusser) would be enchanted by the powerful words printed in those malicious weeklies. Freire argues:

> What lady, jealous of keeping her waist in elegant proportions, wouldn't be seduced by these delicate Regent vests and these elegant shapes from the Escoffon house, Rua da Ajuda n°07, which has perfected them beyond belief? Madame Camille Escoffon asked in an advertisement in the *Jornal do Comercio* of January 21, 1875. She added that: "preserving the waist without compressing it into a narrow vest, tightening the belly without oppressing its flexibility" was the solution. The ideal solution to the problem of Brazilian women having narrow waists - according to European fashion - without suffering too much from this anti-maternal and anti-patriarchal requirement (FREYRE, 1961, p.105).

This moment of erasure in patriarchy will influence women's writing so strongly that it becomes impossible for it to remain the same. Both literature and the media, starting with the written newspaper, will serve as driving forces behind the transformations that take place in writing, and even more so for the advancement of women's writing.

It was in the meantime that, as we said at the beginning, Rachel de Queiroz appeared with her work **O Quinze** and caused a real revolution in the literary world. In Brazil, this female revolution can be seen in the works written by women such as Mary Del Priore, Patricia Galvâo, among others, as well as Rachel de Queiroz. As we have seen, Rachel de Queiroz's first novel opened the door to other novels that demystified the projection of women in environments considered to be reserved only for men.

The fact that Rachel de Queiroz occupied a seat in the Brazilian Academy of Letters in 1977 was not only an event in which a woman conquered a space that had once been denied to her, but also symbolized what happened in women's writing after her, in other words, the breaking of the traditional constraints brought about in the novel, thus linking author and character as two responsible for two important ruptures for Brazilian literature and Brazilian women's writing: the patriarchal tradition of marriage and the patriarchal dominance in Brazilian literature.

FINAL CONSIDERATIONS

I'm not a feminist. I think society has to grow together. The association between women and men is very good and I think it's a big mistake to fight against men. I just dedicate myself more to women's stories, in fact, my main characters are always women (Rachel de Queiroz, Roda viva, TV Cultura, 1991).

Throughout the work we have seen how Rachel de Queiroz tried to exempt herself from the title and stereotype of feminist given to her by others when interpreting her writing and her characters throughout her writing career. In fact, according to the writer herself, it was never her aim to write pieces that spoke out against men, specifically, or patriarchy, in general. Her trajectory, however, always writing stories with a female magnifying glass, meant that others saw her as a feminist, often citing her as an example of a feminist writer, which they did without her endorsement, of course.

The fact that she produced her first novel featuring a character of the nature of Conceiçao makes Rachel's declaration of non-feminism seem like pure *mise-en-scène* on the part of the author. One of her great achievements with **O Quinze** was, as well as working on the issue of breaking with tradition, as we have tried to demonstrate through this work, to critically discuss the problems that the thirties were going through, leaving her indignation and struggle on the pages of the work through the demonstration of altruism by the character Conceiçao. This altruism was expressed by her strong dedication to the victims of the concentration camps.

The book, which reached its 100th edition in 2015[a] , has always "haunted" the writer who, in a 1998 interview with **Folha de Sao Paulo**, ironically stated: "I have a mortal dislike of **O Quinze**, that book has haunted me for 60 years". And this is exactly the book that put her in the spotlight, becoming the subject of numerous studies, including this one.

After all, Conceiçao, the protagonist of the work, will be the first Rachel de Queiroz character to break with the stereotypes imposed on women by the patriarchy, and the work is also the first to create a number of female characters in Queiroz's career who will live independently, free from the cultural and social ties mentioned throughout this work.

On the political front, Rachel always claimed to be a Trotskyist and never shied away from this movement, as she had done with communism. Her influence among Trotskyists was so considerable that:

In Fortaleza, she was advised by the Trotskyists to run for deputy for the Socialist Party, participating in the Frente Única Antifasciste (FUA) along with Stalinist friends like Jeder de Carvalho. This was only possible for two reasons: the first was the universal suffrage and women's candidacy guaranteed by the new Constitution, launched that same year. In addition, the Communist International had changed its orientation due to the rise of Nazism in Germany, and began to see "class collaboration" as a good strategy for fighting the extreme right (GUERELLUS, 2016, p. 220, author's emphasis).

Being nominated for a party ticket shows us how much influence Rachel had in the political arena. At that time, a woman exerting political influence in a circle of men to the point of being nominated for a position of popular representation was not something trivial and, when compared to today, was of unparalleled importance.

As the research dealt with the conquest of space by women, this fact can be seen as another conquest of that space in a wise and perceptive way on the part of the author. Rachel de Queiroz was thus a woman ahead of her time. In September 1998, when she launched her autobiography **Tantos anos** with her sister Maria Luiza, they both gave an interview to reporter Cynara Meneses, who had been sent to Quixadâ. It is in this interview that her sister states that "Rachel's life was more or less parallel to the political life of Brazil. She followed all the movements and took part in them" (MENESES, 1998).

Reading about women's participation in the 1930s in general, about women who lived in bitterness, trapped in an unhappy life in order to satisfy the desires of a patriarchal and domineering society, it is perhaps somewhat perplexing to understand Rachel de Queiroz's resourcefulness in society at that time. Perhaps this resourcefulness is justified by the intellectual life of her parents. Rachel grew up in the midst of books, so much so that, in an interview, the author comments that writing **O Quinze** didn't surprise her parents, because the environment in which she grew up couldn't have produced anything other than the great intellectual she was.

Rachel de Queiroz had all the conditions to experience a traditional family, which was her own. Conceiçao, on the other hand, was brought up in a home without any male reference and her grandmother is the only family reference she knows, since there is no male figure in the girl's upbringing. Her grandmother will then play the role of this patriarchal voice, which censors her all the time, as we saw during our work.

Although the main focus of this research is on breaking with tradition, it has not failed to discuss the female space, women's writing and its specificities in contrast to men's writing. A curious fact that can be observed when it comes to women writers is what Mozambican writer Paulina Chiziane observes when she says that "when men write, people don't call them macho and we women, when we write, are called feminists" (CHIZIANE, 2010, p. 174). This is because Chiziane also shares the same dilemma as Rachel de Queiroz when she doesn't consider herself to be a feminist, nor does she claim to be one, while others try to label her as such. Neither Queiroz nor Chiziane agree with such labels, nor do they weave their writing in such a direction.

The study carried out here, under the aegis of theorists from literature, anthropology and even philosophy, sought to contribute to giving visibility to the strength of women. It therefore sought to explore how Rachel de Queiroz's intellectual apprenticeship was a foretaste of what would happen in 1977, with her appointment to the Brazilian Academy of Letters. In fact, it is believed that this event marked the history of the academy, Brazilian literature and women writers in post-Rachel de Queiroz Brazil forever.

REFERENCES

ABREU, Laile Ribeiro. **Representations in the work of Rachel de Queiroz**. 2016.

273 f. Thesis (Doctorate in Brazilian Literature). Faculty of Letters, UFMG, Belo Horizonte, 2016.

ALENCAR, José de. **Senhora**. Sâo Paulo: Editora Martin Claret Ltda, 2006.

ALMEIDA, José Américo de. **A bagaceira**. 12. ed. Rio de Janeiro: José Olympio, 1972.

ALMEIDA, Thiago de; CENTEVILLE, Valéria. **Romantic jealousy and its relationship with violence.** Psych. Rev. Sâo Paulo, volume 16, n.1 and n.2, 73-91, 2007.

ALTHUSSER, Louis. **Ideology and ideological apparatuses of the** state. **Lisbon: Presença, 1974.**

AMADO, Jorge. **Seara vermelha:** novel. Sâo Paulo: Record, 1982.

AMADO, Jorge. **Dead Sea.** Sâo Paulo: Companhia das Letras, 2008.

AMADO, Jorge. **Capitâes da areia**. Sâo Paulo: Companhia de Bolso, 2011.

ANDRADE, Carlos Drummond. **O sentimento do mundo.** 12. ed Rio de Janeiro: Record, 2001.

ARROJO, Rosemary. **Oficina de traduçâo**: a teoria na pràtica. 5. ed. Sâo Paulo: Atica, 2007.

ASSIS, Joaquim Maria Machado de. **Esaù e Jacó.** 5. ed. Sâo Paulo: Martin Claret, 2012.

AZEVEDO, Aluisio. **O cortiço.** Sâo Paulo: Abril cultural, 1981.

AZEVEDO, Aluisio. **The man.** Rio de Janeiro: Paris: Livraria Garnier, 1887.

AZEVEDO, Aluisio. **Pension house.** Sâo Paulo: DCL, 2013.

BACHOFEN, J. (1987). **El Matiarcado.** Madrid: Akal (Original published in 1861).

BADINTER, Elisabeth. **A love conquered: The myth of maternal love.** 5. ed. Rio de Janeiro: Editora Nova Fronteira, 1985.

BAMISILE, Adetunji Sunday. **Gender issues and women's writing in contemporary African literature and African diaspora.** Lisbon, 2012.

BEAUVOIR, Simone de. **The second sex.** Rio de Janeiro: Nova Fronteira, 1970.

BOSI, Alfredo. **Heaven, hell:** essays in literary and ideological criticism. Sao Paulo: Atica, 1988.

BOURDIEU, Pierre. **Male domination.** 10. ed. Rio de Janeiro: Bertrand Brasil, 2011.

BRAIT, Beth. **The character**. Sao Paulo: Atica, 1985.

BRANCO, Lucia Castelo. **What is women's writing**? Sao Paulo: Editora Brasiliense, 1991.

BRAZIL. Regional Labor Court. 24ª Regiao. **Creation of the CLT**. Available at :https://trt-24.jusbrasil.com.br/noticias/100474551/historia-a-criacao-da-clt.

Accessed on: 09 July, 2017.

CÀNDIDO, Antônio. **A educação pela noite e outros ensaios.** Sao Paulo: Atica, 1987.

CANDIDO, Antônio. **A personagem de ficçâo.** 2nd ed. Sao Paulo: Perspectiva, 1968.

CANDIDO, Antônio. **Literature and society.** 8. ed. Sao Paulo: T. A. Queiroz, 2000.

COSTA, Naiara Lauriene. Souza; RIBEIRO, Horta Gilman; BRASIL, Deilton Ribeiro. **The Code of Manu: main aspects.** Journal of Law, Politics and Philosophy, Conselheiro Lafaiete Law School. V. 2, year III, Aug. - Dec 2014.

COULEVAIN, Pierre de. **In uncertainty**. Translated by Jorge Gonçalves. Rio de Janeiro: Flores e Mano Editores, 1930.

COUTO, Mia. **The construction of Mia Couto**. 2017.

Available at:

<http://www.otempo.com.br/divers%C3%A3o/magazine/aconstru%C3%A7%C3 %A3 o-de-mia-couto-1.1490967> Accessed: 01 July 2017.

CURY, Augusto Jorge, **Dez leis para ser feliz: ferramentas para se apaixonar pela vida.** Rio de Janeiro: Sextante, 2003.

DEL PRIORE, Mary. (org.) *et al.,* **História das mulheres no Brasil.** Sao Paulo: Ed. Contexto, 1997.

DUARTE, Constância Lima; DUARTE, Eduardo de Assis; BEZERRA, Katia da Costa (Org.) **Gènero e representação na Literatura Brasileira**. Belo Horizonte: Editora UFMG. 2002.

DUARTE, Constância Lima (Org.) **Arquivos femininos**: Literatura, valores,

senses. Florianópolis: Editora mulheres, 2014.

DUARTE, Constância Lima. **Women and writing: literary production and female emancipation in Brazil.** Journal of the Postgraduate Program in Cultural Criticism, Bahia State University, Campus II - Alagoinhas, undated.

DUARTE, Constância Lima. **Fragmented femininity.** Ipotesi Magazine. Juiz de Fora, v. 13, n. 2, p. 31 - 37 jul./dez. 2009.

DUARTE, Constância Lima. **Women's literature and literary criticism.** Paper presented at ANPOLL - II National Meeting, May 26-29, 1987. Rio de Janeiro.

ENGELS, Friedrich. **The Origin of the Family, Private Property and the State.** Rio de Janeiro: Vitória, 1964.

FERREIRA, Lara Vanessa de Castro, **Enxadas e compassos, seca, ciência e trabalho no sertâo cearense.** 2009. 153 f. Master's dissertation. Federal University of Bahia, Faculty of Philosophy and Human *Sciences*. Salvador, *2009.* Available at:<file:///C:/Users/escritorio/Downloads/2009%20lara.pdf> Accessed: March 03, 2017.

FREYRE, Gilberto. **Sobrados e mucambos: decadência do patriarcado rural no Brasil.** Sâo Paulo: Comp. Ed. Nacional, 1961.

FRIEDAN, Betty**. Feminine mysticism**. Translated by Aurea B. Weissenberg. Rio de Janeiro: Vozes Publishers, 1971.

GALVÂO, Patricia. **Industrial park.** Rio de Janeiro: J. Olympio, 2006.

GAMBARATO, Renira Rampazzo. **Sign, meaning, representation.** Revista Contemporânea, Sâo Paulo, n. 4, 2005.

GUERELLUS, Natâlia de Santana. **Rachel de Queiroz politica**: uma escrita entre esquerdas e diretas no Brasil (1910-1964). Curitiba, 2008.

HOUAISS, Antônio. **Houaiss Dictionary of the Portuguese Language**. 2. Ed. Rio de Janeiro, Ed. Objetiva, 2004.

MADEIRA, Vagner Martins. **Machado de Assis: Homem lùdico, uma leitura de Esaù e Jacó.** Sâo Paulo: Annablume Publishing House, 2001.

MAIA, Clàudia de Jesus. **A invençâo da solteirona**: **conjugalidade moderna e terror moral** - Minas Gerais (1890-1948), UNB-ICH, Brasilia, 2007.

MENESES, Cynara. **Rachel de Queiroz interviewed by Folha in 1998.** Folha Online. Available at:

<http://www1.folha.uol.com.br/folha/ilustrada/ult90u38515.shtml> Accessed 05 Jul 2017.

MOREIRA, Maria de Fâtima Salum**. Men and women in the 30s:**

social tensions and everyday life. Revista de Ciências humanas, Florianópolis, v. 15, n°21 p.23-35, 1997.

MOREIRA, Terezinha Taborda. **Silence and trauma in Paulina Chiziane's women's writing.** Women and Literature Magazine - vol. 17 - 2nd quarter - 2016.

Available at: <http://litcult.net/silencio-e-trauma-na-escrita-literaria-de-paulina-chiziane-terezinha-taborda-moreira/>

NARVAZ, Marta Giudice. **Submission and resistance: Exploding the patriarchal discourse of female domination.** 2005. 195f. Rio Grande do Sul: Federal University of Rio Grande do Sul, Postgraduate Course in Developmental Psychology. Porto Alegre, 2005.

NIETZSCHE, Friedrich Wilhelm. **The Antichrist.** Translated by L&PM Editores. Rio de Janeiro: L&PM Pocket, 2008.

NORDAU, Max Simon. **The conventional lies of our civilization.** 2nd.

ed. Lisbon: Typ. de Francisco Luiz Gonçalves, 1911. (Biblioteca da Educaçâo Nacional).

PEREIRA JÛNIOR, Edilson Alves. **Space, Industrialization and Capitalist Accumulation: an approach to the Northeast and Cearà** In. Mercator - Revista de Geografia da UFC, year 02, number 04, p 65 -76. 2003.

QUEIROZ, Rachel de. **Caminho** de **pedras**. 8. ed. Rio de Janeiro: Editora José Olympio, 1985.

QUEIROZ, Rachel de. **Joao Miguel**. 9. ed. São Paulo: Editora Siciliano, 1992.

QUEIROZ, Rachel de; QUEIROZ, Maria Luiza de. **Tantos anos**. Sâo Paulo: Siciliano, 1998.

QUEIROZ, Rachel de. **The Fifteen**. 100. ed. Rio de Janeiro: Editora José Olympio, 2015.

QUEIROZ, Rachel de. **Speech by Rachel de Queiroz at the inauguration of the ABL.** Available at: <http://www.academia.org.br/academicos/rachel-de-

queiroz/discurso- de-posse Accessed on Feb 10, 2017.

QUEIROZ, Rachel. **Interview with** Rachel de Queiroz. Roda Viva. Available at: <http://www.rodaviva.fapesp.br/materia/407/entrevistados/rachel_de_queiroz_199 1.h tm> Accessed on Feb. 10, 2017.

QUEIROZ, Rachel. **Caderno de Literatura Brasileira do Instituto Moreira Sales.**

QUEIROZ, Rachel. **Inaugural speech**. Available at: <http://www.academia.org.br/academicos/rachel-de-queiroz/discurso-de-posse>

RAMOS, Diana dos Santos. **Memory and advertising in Brazil in the**

1930. 2013. 169f. Rio de Janeiro: UNIRIO, Graduate Program in Social Memory, 2013.

RAMOS, Graciliano. **Sâo Bernardo**. 66. ed. 5.v. Rio de Janeiro: Record, 1996. RAMOS,

Graciliano. **Vidas secas.** 131. ed. Rio de Janeiro: Record, 2016.

RAMOS, Graciliano. **Crooked lines**. Sâo Paulo: Record, 1980.

RÊGO, José Lins do. **Banguê**. 12ª ed. Rio de Janeiro: J. Olympio, 1980.

RENAN, Ernest. **The Life of Jesus.** Translated by Eliana Maria de A. Martins. Sâo Paulo: Editora Martins Claret, 2004.

RIBEIRO, Cristiane Felipe. As pontas de uma estrala: poetics of silence in Macabéa and Ponciâ. Belo Horizonte, 2016.

RUFINO, Maria Beatriz Cruz. **Industrial Development and Spatial Organization**: Some considerations on the Metropolitan Region of Fortaleza. Faculty of Architecture and Urbanism, University of São Paulo, August, 2008.

SAMARA, Eni Mesquita**. The mysteries of human fragility**. Brazilian Magazine of History. V. 15, n° 29, p. 57-71. Sâo Paulo, 1995.

SCHOLZE Lia. **Women in Literature**: **gender and representation.** In: DUARTE, Constância Lima; DUARTE, Eduardo de Assis; BEZERRA, Kâtia da Costa (Org.) **Gênero e representaçâo na Literatura Brasileira.** Belo Horizonte: Editora UFMG. 2002.

SCHWANTES, Cintia**. Dilemmas of female representation.** Opsis - Revista do NIESC, Distrito federal, vol. 6, p. 7-19, 2006.

SHIKO**, Adaptation for comics of the work of Rachel de Queiroz**. Sâo Paulo: Atica, 2012.

SPIVAK, Gayatri Chakravorty. **Can the subaltern speak?** Translated by Sandra Regina Goulart Almeida, Marcos Pereira Feitosa, André Pereira Feitosa. Belo Horizonte: Editora UFMG, 2010.

VERISSIMO, Érico. **Cross roads**. Rio de Janeiro: Globo, 1953.

WOOLF, Virginia; FROES, Leonardo. **The value of laughter and other essays.** Sâo Paulo: Cosac Naify, 2014.

WOOLF, Virginia; Translation: RIBEIRO, Vera. **A roof all your own.** Rio de Janeiro: Nova Fronteira, 1985.

ANNEXES

Photo 01 - Cover of the first edition of O quinze (1930)

Source: Good News Agency website

Available at: http://www.boanoticia.org.br/um-novo-olhar-sobre-o-quinze-de-rachel-de-queiroz

Photo 02 - Cover of the 100th edition of *O quinze* (2015) (Main edition used during the writing of the dissertation)

Source: <https://www.saraiva.com.br/>

Photo 03 - Comic book edition of *The Fifteen,* by Shiko (2012)

Source: <http://www.raiolaser.net/2012/08/tons-da-seca.html>

Photo 04 - Rachel receives the Queen of Students award (1929)

Source: Instituto Moreira Salles living collection

Available at: <https://ims.com.br/por-dentro-acervos/acervo-vivo>

Photo 05 - Fazenda do Pici, where Rachel wrote O quinze in 1930

Source: Blog Inventàrio Ambiental

Fortaleza Available from: <http://inventarioambientalfortaleza.blogspot.com.br/search?q=rachel+de+queiroz>

Photo 06 - Rachel de Queiroz (Photo by Edu Simoes-1997)

Source: Blog Tamires de Carvalho

Available at: <http://www.tamiresdecarvalho.com/letras-rachel-de-queiroz-sobre-o-amor-e- academia-brasileira-de-letras>

Photo 07 - Rachel de Queiroz receiving the cord from José Américo de Almeida on the day of her inauguration to chair no. 05 at the ABL - 1977

Source: Templo Cultural Delfos website

Photo 08 - Ceremony on the day he took up his seat at the ABL - 1977

Source: Slide Player website

Available at: <http://slideplayer.com.br/slide/10858808/>

Photo 09 - Inauguration speech at the ABL - 1977

Source: Templo Cultural Delfos website

Photo 10 - Immortals of the ABL

Source: Blog Jornal O povo

Available at: <http://blogs.opovo.com.br/leiturasdabel/2017/08/03/em-1977

MIX
Papier aus verantwortungsvollen Quellen
Paper from responsible sources
FSC® C105338

FSC
www.fsc.org

Printed by Books on Demand GmbH, Norderstedt / Germany